BISON
BOOKS

The Life *of the* Afterlife *in the* Big Sky State

A History of Montana's Cemeteries

ELLEN BAUMLER

University of Nebraska Press
Lincoln

Acknowledgments for the use of copyrighted material appear
on pages xix–xx, which constitute an extension of
the copyright page.

Publication of this book is made possible in part by generous
support from the Montana History Foundation.

MF

THE MONTANA HISTORY
FOUNDATION

Library of Congress Cataloging-in-Publication Data
Names: Baumler, Ellen, author.
Title: The life of the afterlife in the Big Sky State : a history of
Montana's cemeteries / Ellen B. Baumler.
Other titles: History of Montana's cemeteries
Description: Lincoln : University of Nebraska Press, [2021] |
Includes bibliographical references and index.
Identifiers: LCCN 2020041728
ISBN 9781496214805 (paperback)
ISBN 9781496226938 (epub)
ISBN 9781496226945 (mobi)
ISBN 9781496226952 (pdf)
Subjects: LCSH: Cemeteries—Montana—History. | Funeral rites and
ceremonies—Montana—History. | Burial—Montana—History.
Classification: LCC GT3210.M9 B38 2021 | DDC 393.09786—dc23
LC record available at https://lccn.loc.gov/2020041728

Set in New Baskerville ITC Pro by Laura Buis.

Frontispiece: An open scroll and lilies winding around a tree trunk
ornament the tombstone of Eliza Jane Parke at Hillside Cemetery
in Virginia City. Photograph by Larry Goldsmith.

What is life? It is the flash of a firefly in the night. It is the breath of a buffalo in the wintertime. It is the little shadow that runs across the grass and loses itself in the sunset.

—ISAPO-MUXIKA (Crowfoot), Siksika chief (1830–90)

Contents

List of Illustrations ix

Preface. xi

Acknowledgments. xix

Chapter 1. Death and Burial among the First Montanans 1

Chapter 2. Mortuary Customs of the Upper Missouri Tribes . . . 13

Chapter 3. Tragedy beyond Description 23

Chapter 4. Before There Was Billings 33

Chapter 5. Conflict, Misfortune, and Uneasy Transitions. 42

Chapter 6. Death in Montana's Early Communities. 59

Chapter 7. Dead and Buried Twice. 79

Chapter 8. The Evolution of Beautiful Burial Grounds. 91

Chapter 9. Cemetery Diversity 105

Chapter 10. Homage to the Dead 127

Chapter 11. How We Miss Them 141

Afterword 161

Notes. 163

Bibliographic Essay 177

Index. 181

Illustrations

1. Anzick Site, Park County 2
2. Excavations at Pictograph Cave 9
3. *The Last Scene of the Last Act of the Sioux War,* 1891 wood
   engraving 16
4. Blackfeet burial, Glacier National Park 19
5. Grave at Sacred Heart Catholic Cemetery, Fort Belknap 21
6. Blackfeet grave, Blackfeet Reservation 31
7. Freighter's outfit near Coulson, 1882 35
8. Face on the Rims 36
9. Tree burials 38
10. J. J. Crittenden headboard, Little Bighorn Battlefield 48
11. Horse and human bones, Little Bighorn Battlefield 50
12. Grave of James McGuire, Big Hole Battlefield 55
13. Cowboy's funeral 60
14. Salish cemetery, St. Mary's Mission 64
15. Bannack overview 68
16. "New" Bannack cemetery 69
17. Aboveground crypt, Virginia City 72
18. Bird's-eye view of Helena, 1875 74
19. Children's tombstone at Elkhorn 76
20. Bird's-eye view of Missoula, 1884 81
21. Coffin hardware 83
22. Metal casket unearthed at Clancy 86
23. A. K. Prescott signature 96
24. The Fairy Steps 103
25. Funerary burner at Mount Moriah Cemetery, Butte 111

26. Japanese tombstone at Hillcrest Cemetery, Deer Lodge . . . 114

27. Custer National Cemetery 121

28. Section marker, Warm Springs 125

29. Funeral of Plenty Coups 130

30. Funeral of C. M. Russell 132

31. Mine memorial, Mountain View Cemetery, Butte 133

32. Victim retrieval, Mann Gulch 135

33. Shep, *Ever Faithful*, Fort Benton 138

34. MacDonald family cemetery, Fort Connah 144

35. Frank Little grave, Mountain View Cemetery, Butte 150

36. Portrait tombstone, Bearcreek Cemetery 152

37. Wooden crosses, Mayn Cemetery, White Sulphur Springs . . 154

38. Wimsett monument, Mountain View Cemetery, Columbus . . 156

39. Delicate fencing, Hillcrest Cemetery, Deer Lodge 158

40. White cross on Montana roadway 160

Preface

Nothing awakens our senses like a walk through a cemetery. Whether those who sleep in eternal rest are family, or friends, or strangers, cemeteries capture the most powerful human expressions of love, of loss, and of harsh reality. Cemeteries are extraordinary tools that teach us about life, its richness, its shortcomings, its dangers, and its lofty emotions. Cemeteries can be compelling and evocative for their exquisite, haunting beauty, but they can also represent stark, painful, ugly truths.

I have always enjoyed cemeteries for their solitude, their diversity, and the stories I can learn from them. However, the opportunity to research, write, and teach about them did not present itself until some thirty years ago when my career as a Montana historian led me to interpret such places. Since then, I have authored National Register of Historic Places nominations and interpretive plaques for cemeteries across Montana. I have written stories about them, and I have led hundreds of enthusiastic locals and visitors of all ages on many cemetery tours in various communities. I have encountered firsthand profound energy in places of the dead and observed how this energy influences and sometimes energizes the living. I have also experienced heavy sadness in places that have been ignored and neglected.

The Life of the Afterlife is about Montana's beautiful, tended cemeteries where we can experience art and history, and about how we remember those whose footprints survive only in our memories: a child's chair carved in marble, a lamb resting on a bed of stone, a child's portrait looking over a final resting place, eternally preserved yet hauntingly vibrant. White crosses on the highways, the Granite Mountain memorial with its lovely and terrible facsimiles, and the tearstained Face on the Rims overlooking Billings speak to remembrance. But the chapters herein are also about the lost, the missing, the misplaced, and the rediscovered that I have encountered along the varied pathways of my career.

I learned firsthand about the missing and misplaced when I wrote about Celestia Alice Earp in *Beyond Spirit Tailings* in 2005. She was shot five times as she rode a stage from Red Bluff to Virginia City trying to escape a spurned suitor. He was subsequently hanged for her murder. I never discovered where she was buried even though her death was well covered in the press.

Celestia lingered in agony, fully conscious, for many hours. She settled her affairs and requested burial in Ohio next to her husband, Richard. There is, however, no record of her interment there. During territorial days, marked graves were not the norm, and this is a case in point. There were no tombstone makers in Montana until the late 1870s. Tombstones had to be ordered by mail from the local hardware store. Further, until the advent of the Northern Pacific Railway in 1883, freighting was prohibitively expensive, especially for heavy items like marble, and transit took months.

Nearly a century after Celestia's death in 1965, a Main Street business in Bozeman was undergoing some renovations. Owners had long been aware of an odd protrusion in the basement floor. During installation of some new plumbing, the bump in the floor turned out to be Celestia's marble tombstone. A fire in the mid-1880s had destroyed a hardware store on the site and the heavy tombstone must have fallen through the floor to the basement. Celestia's sister, her only relative in Montana, had returned to Ohio by the end of 1881, and the tombstone went unclaimed. The epitaph read:

CELESTIA

Wife of

RICHARD J. EARP

Died

Mar. 26, 1881

Aged

32 Y. 12 D.

Dearest Celestia thou has left us

Here thy loss we deeply feel

But 'tis God that hath bereft us

He can all our sorrows heal

The tombstone found its way into the Caroline McGill collection, which eventually became the foundation for the Museum of the Rockies. At some point, the tombstone was either lost or misplaced. The location of Celestia's final resting place, whether in Montana or in Ohio, remains speculative, although since the tombstone ended up in Montana, that is likely where she was buried.

Families sometimes replace old tombstones and they become decorations in rock gardens or steppingstones in backyards. Sometimes tombstones are discarded when development encroaches. Occasionally a found marker can be returned to its intended place. I once had a call about a missing tombstone discovered in an alley on Helena's West Side. Research into the name and date of death on the marker led me to the Home of Peace, Helena's historic Jewish cemetery. In the 1930s, the local newspaper reported that the cemetery had been vandalized and this tombstone stolen. Because the cemetery caretakers kept careful plot maps (not always the case), the person's grave was located and the tombstone, missing for more than half a century, was reset in its rightful place.

Derelict and forgotten historic cemeteries are no less compelling than their grand, elegant cousins, but draw upon opposite emotions. Neglected cemeteries are especially melancholy and depressing. Montana, unfortunately, has a number of these. Most heart-wrenching of all is the vast cemetery at Warm Springs State

Hospital, dating back to the late 1870s. It is especially poignant because of its massive anonymity. Fields of hundreds of graves represent human potential lost to tuberculosis, dementia, suicide, and myriad other terrible causes. The graves lie silent, cast away and forgotten, with nothing to recall once-living individuals who have now turned to dust. Bleak wooden section markers, warped with age and exposure, are the only indication that the areas have seen use. Unless you walk through the sections carefully, you miss the occasional rusted mortuary tags with typed and illegible names. Hiking through those fields hits you in the gut; the sheer enormity of it is incomprehensible.

While we might admonish the founding physicians and staff at Warm Springs, they too, were human and surely faced some insurmountable difficulties. Longtime physician Dr. Armistead Mitchell, a principal founder of Warm Springs and one of its longtime administrators and physicians, was a well-respected family man despite what some would say about the conditions and treatment of his patients at Warm Springs.

Dr. Mitchell was a rough-and-tumble, widely traveled gold rush doctor and successful miner who had already made a fortune before he and Dr. Charles F. Mussigbrod founded Warm Springs. Among the famous cases in his early repertoire was the amputation of a man's arm with a butcher knife, a common saw, and whisky as anesthetic in a Bear Town saloon. Three planks between whiskey barrels served as the operating table. "Shorty," the patient, had fallen into a fire and burned his arm to a crisp. After the surgery, Shorty ordered drinks all around.

Despite a reputation as a physician with a brusque bedside manner, Dr. Mitchell had a soft heart. Researching his family members who are buried at Hillcrest Cemetery in Deer Lodge, I came across a most poignant little story about him. In 1893 when Dr. Mitchell's son, Hugh, was away at business college in Chicago, he suddenly became ill. The parents reached his bedside just before Hugh died. Dr. Mitchell brought him home to Deer Lodge for burial as he had requested. Several years later, when the family dog died, Dr. Mitchell—despite suffering from mastoiditis, a painful terminal illness—brought the body to Deer

Lodge. He had a small place dug at the foot of his son's grave and buried the dog there. "Ike" had been his son's cherished companion. Although Ike's burial place is unmarked, it is somehow comforting to know he is there. My respect for Dr. Mitchell has grown considerably.

I have learned the value of rediscovery. In 2008 I had the good fortune to accompany a group of ninth graders and Cheryl Hughes, their enthusiastic, innovative English teacher, on what was to be the first of many memorable field trips. At the old Jocko Agency on the Flathead Reservation several miles southeast of Arlee, the students' task on this day was to tidy up the unassuming historic cemetery where notable Salish families and chiefs had long been buried. Cautioned to leave items and tokens at the individual graves untouched, the students weeded, took notes, and explored. It was in the cemetery sometime later, at Cheryl's introduction, that I first met the venerated Salish elder Louis Adams. He gathered us in the lovely St. John Berchmans Catholic Church adjacent and we all listened intently as Louis, in his quiet way, shared inspirational stories of family, loss, and renewed hope. It was a profound experience for all of us.

A few field trips later in May 2012 in the Bitterroot Selway wilderness, Louis and his daughter Arleen accompanied us to Nez Perce Pass. They led the students up a steep slope, to a remote ridge high above the pass on the Montana-Idaho border. On this ridge in 1975, Louis and Arleen had rediscovered the grave of Louis's great-great-grandfather, Francis "Plassie" Adams. Plassie had died in 1900 on a trip through the Selway and was buried there.

On that May day in 2012, a highly charged, emotional event unfolded. A light rain fell, casting a somber shadow over the mountain meadow that had yet to burst with the first growth of spring. As the students stood reverent atop the steep hill, Arleen and Louis sang an honor song over the grave of their ancestor; their strong blended voices carried on the wind. Both Louis and his daughter, and some of the students, were moved to tears. Louis later acknowledged that he had not realized the importance of this rediscovery until that afternoon. Reconnecting with ancestors and associated traditions, or experiencing such an event for the first time, can lead to personal renewal. I think all who were present would agree that these themes—rediscovery and renewal—intertwine in the places where the souls of those who came before us are at rest.

Sometimes the dead truly do speak to us in ways we cannot explain. I know this from personal experience. On a brilliantly sunny spring day in May 2012, I had led sixty Helena fourth graders on a history field trip, finishing the day at Benton Avenue Cemetery. Teachers let the students freely explore. As I stood with a few parents in the central roadway, three visibly shaken students came running. They claimed to have seen the apparition of a teenager in a yellow dress sitting under a tree at the cemetery's north edge. Upon investigation, a parent found the grave of fifteen-year-old Fern Marie Wilson near the tree. Extensive research uncovered Fern's sad story, which ended—or maybe didn't end—with her suicide in 1911.

The discovery inspired me to write about Fern. My story was nearly finished the following year when I invited a psychic friend to visit Fern's grave with me. I wanted to see if she could verify the information I had collected. She did, in fact, and added one further detail: Fern was wearing a yellow dress, but she also wore a lovely lace collar over it.

Again on a fine day in May 2013, another group of sixty fourth graders, with the same teachers but different students, had spent the day with me. Ending at the cemetery, the teachers asked me to tell the kids about Fern but not to scare them by including many details. It was no surprise when some twenty kids made a beeline for the tree. A while later, some of them claimed to have seen Fern. I thought they were kidding until they began to describe what they had seen, and one girl said to me, "She had on a yellow dress, but she had this beautiful lace collar over it." Only my psychic friend and I knew that detail.

The teacher called time and as we headed to the gate, another student fell in step with me. He looked shaken and finally spoke, "That was the freakiest thing I have ever seen. I saw her too," he said, "and I will never forget it. She was looking straight ahead, and her face was gray, but her mouth was white and well, sort of *pinched*." I had not told them that Fern committed suicide by drinking carbolic acid and in her gruesome death throes, her mouth was white with burns.

I cannot deny these uncanny coincidences. Fern made her presence known, twice, and obviously wanted her story to be told. I obliged, telling it fully in my book, *Haunted Helena.*

Cemeteries offer us varied and sometimes unusual opportunities. While collecting information on a National Register nomination for Kalispell's C. E. Conrad Memorial Cemetery, the sexton introduced me to its legendary Fairy Steps. He led me down the beautiful stone stairway with its switchbacks that end at the remnants of a tree-lined carriage path along the Stillwater River. Mrs. Conrad had the steps cut into the hillside in the early 1900s so that she could privately visit her husband's grave. Generations of children have since scampered up and down the steps. Legend has it that when you go up and down and count the hundred-or-so stairs, you will never get the same number twice. I counted them myself, and both times ended up with different numbers. I hardly scampered, and confess that the climb is long, steep, and so exhausting that one simply cannot keep an accurate count. The steps, however, are one of Montana's most beautiful well-kept secrets.

It has taken many years to collect these photographs, biographies, and histories of cemeteries and grave sites across Montana. The state has more than 1,750 formally identified cemeteries and thousands upon thousands of undiscovered attendant stories. Every community has its own cemetery history, and each one is just as significant as the other. This small volume is not intended to recount the deeds of the famous, nor can it be in any way comprehensive. However, I hope that it will appeal to those who love history, and quiet places, and wandering among the dead. Perhaps it will inspire visits to local cemeteries and lead to stories waiting to be told. And perhaps, the dead will speak to you, too.

Acknowledgments

Mention of all those whose paths have crossed mine in the more than two decades I have spent collecting information for this work would be impossible, but there are a few whose support and assistance I especially want to credit.

Charleen Spalding has been my friend and "cemetery mentor" since we met many years ago. Her work has been meticulous and inspiring. She and her son, Ric Seabrook, have documented nearly every cemetery in Lewis and Clark, Broadwater, and Jefferson counties. She is a true graveyard detective, always willing and eager to take up a difficult thread and ferret out the truth. Charleen is always generous with her research. She has not only been willing to share information, but she goes out of her way to add facts to my own discoveries. She helped plant the seed of this present work with the publication of her own important work, *Benton Avenue Cemetery: A Pioneer Resting Place.*

I am grateful to the Montana Historical Society for allowing me the leeway throughout my career to go beyond my job description, researching cemeteries and writing National Register nominations for several of them. Together with my supervisor, Kirby Lambert, and colleague, Deb Mitchell, we were able to bring expert gravestone restorer Jonathon Appell from Connecticut to Montana three times to conduct workshops and repairs on needy cemeteries across the state. These experiences furthered my passion for the subject and the need for a historical perspective on the afterlife in the Treasure State. Charlene Porsild of the Montana History Foundation also deserves credit for taking up this cause and stimulating statewide interest in cemetery preservation, funding many small cemetery projects through the foundation's grant program.

Thanks to my good friend and colleague Jon Axline for sharing my enthusiasm for cemeteries and encouraging me in the project. As the author of the National Register nomination for the Bearcreek Cemetery and a reviewer of my initial manuscript, I am grateful for his insights, perspectives, and criticisms, and for generously contributing several of the photographs in this book. Thanks also to Brian Shovers for valuable critiques of the draft manuscript, and I am indebted to Sheriff Craig Doolittle and Larry Goldsmith for contributing several key photographs.

I can never repay my dear friend Cheryl Hughes of Missoula for allowing me to accompany her and her Sentinel High School students on numerous field trips from the Jocko Agency Cemetery to the grave of Francis "Plassie" Adams, high in the remote Selway wilderness. Her willingness to include me in these adventures enriched my knowledge of Montana and its Native people. Most importantly, it afforded me the privilege of knowing the late Salish elder Louis Adams and hearing his family stories firsthand.

This has been a long journey, and Dr. Clark Whitehorn of the University of Nebraska Press has steadfastly been in it with me from the very beginning. In fact, it was he who first suggested such a book, and I appreciate him for sticking with it over the years, advocating for me and my work, believing in this project, and seeing it through. I am also indebted to the skilled editorial staff at the press for their patience and professionalism.

And thanks to our daughter, Katie, for reading the first few chapters and taking up the topic some years ago as a student in anthropology at the University of Montana. Her work led to discoveries about Missoula's early interment history. Special thanks to my husband, Mark, for traipsing around in cemeteries across the state, in snow, rain, and heat, searching for names and signatures, which he was good at finding. I am grateful to him also for lending his professional expertise as an archaeologist with a critical eye in the reading of the first chapter on Montana's earliest history.

The Life *of the* Afterlife *in the* Big Sky State

ONE

Death and Burial among the First Montanans

The Anzick Child

In the dim past, when mammoths roamed a landscape scarred by recently melted glaciers, someone lay a small child to final rest. Loving hands ceremoniously dusted the little boy's remains with red ochre and lay precious heirlooms, also painted with red ochre and closely packed together, on top of the small body. Tucked into a rock shelter overlooking the harsh, expansive landscape, there he lay with his inheritance, undisturbed for thousands of years.

A mile south of Wilsall in present-day Park County, Montana, in 1968, Ben Hargis dug into a slope of fragmented rock debris with his front-end loader. As he cut deep into a weathered sandstone outcrop, he noted a large, shiny, different-colored rock that fell into the bucket. Hargis and his co-worker Calvin Sarver recognized it as a large stone tool. They further investigated the area and found other artifacts covered in "red stuff." Leaving the area to work elsewhere, they returned later that evening with their wives. The four sifted by hand through the fine material on the slope and removed dozens of stone tools and what would later be identified as weathered human cranial fragments. All were covered in red ochre, a mineral pigment commonly associated with ancient burials.

The color red and burials saturated in ochre form a common thread among early human burials in the Baltic, Europe, Britain, Spain, Israel, New Zealand, and myriad other places. Most anthropologists agree that modern humans likely entered the New World via the Bering Land Bridge that connected Siberia

1. The Anzick Site near Wilsall in Park County was discovered in the outcrop, right of center, in 1968. Photograph by Troy Helmick.

and Alaska at least fifteen thousand years ago. Some cultural practices, like the use of ochre, came with these early people. In fact, ochre is the red pigment used thousands of years later to create the red pictographs on cliff walls and in caves. Nearly half a century after the random, ochre-covered Montana discovery, the site—named for the landowner, Mel Anzick—has yielded astonishing scientific information and fueled cultural controversy.[1]

Most recently radiocarbon-dated to between 10,980 to 11,350 years ago, the Paleoindian grave site not only represents Montana's first known burial, it also yielded the only Clovis period skeletal remains yet to be discovered in the New World. Clovis culture was among the earliest in the western hemisphere. The first tools of these earliest people were discovered in 1932 in Clovis, New Mexico, hence the term "Clovis." Their exquisite stone weapons have since been found across the United States. Their fine spear points indicate hunting prowess and capability of bringing down very large prey. Clovis tools span a millennium

and then curiously their weapons disappear from the archaeological record. Theories for their disappearance include climatic
changes that affected their food source and hunting to extinction the animals that assured survival.[2]

While DNA taken from the incomplete cranial fragments of the
Anzick child could not disclose cause of death or health-related
details, what it did reveal added most significantly to the history
of early New World inhabitants. The sample showed a one- to two-
year-old male descended from Asian—not European—ancestors.
His Asian ancestry thus supports the migration theory that Pre-
Clovis people arrived from Asia via the Beringian "land bridge"
that once connected Siberia to present-day Alaska. Migratory
groups may have then followed the coastline or the ice-free corridor that ran south through what is now the Rocky Mountain
Front. Fossilized *Bison antiquus* bone from this corridor dates to
thirteen thousand years ago, further supporting the migration
theory that the corridor provided an avenue for the movement of
animals and people. The boy's genome, or complete set of DNA,
is the oldest recovered in North America and links his ancestry
to descendent indigenous American populations.[3]

Some believe that the spectacular Anzick Site artifacts, on
display at the Montana Historical Society in Helena, comprise
a "toolkit" of utilitarian implements in various stages of manu-
facture. Beautifully fluted Clovis projectile points are the cen-
terpiece, but there are also some seventy flaked stone bifaces,
cores, scrapers, blades, and half a dozen long pieces of bone or
antler. The latter may be atlatl arrow foreshafts or pressure flak-
ers used to sharpen tool edges. Some of the artifacts, several hundred years older than the grave itself, had seen use; others were
new when placed with the remains.

The toolkit includes everything a hunter-gatherer would need
to survive and serves as a visual "how-to" manual. Further, pro-
tein analysis revealed rabbit blood mixed with the ochre to produce a lasting pigment. Two tools also tested positive for rabbit's
blood and a third tested positive for camel (*Camelops hesternus*).
The significance of camel's blood on the artifact is twofold. Its
presence substantiates the time period since *Camelops hesternus*

became extinct after the Pleistocene, or ice age, and it also proves that the assemblage was a real working toolkit. The used, new, and unfinished tools functioned as an heirloom burial assemblage and their covering in red ochre—the oldest pigment known to man—is indicative of ritual activity. Supplying this child in death with everything needed for survival is evidence of belief in an afterlife.[4]

Iron Jaw Wilcox Site

Moving forward to less than two thousand years ago, on a terrace along a creek in present-day Rosebud County, someone dug a shallow pit, placed a male body there and loosely covered it with rocks. The remains were intentionally left partially exposed. There were neither grave goods nor ochre associated with the burial. In the 1960s, BLM employee Gaylon Wilcox reported finding a bone protruding from this low terrace on a primitive access road along Iron Jaw Creek. Archaeologists later determined that twenty sandstone rocks, although somewhat scattered when the road was cut through, had comprised the cairn that marked the grave. This semi-open cairn burial resembles others of the period on the Northwestern Plains and the individual's bone structure is consistent with individuals of Native American ancestry. Radiocarbon dating determined that the individual lived 1,790 years before present. Severe arthritis and loss of all his teeth suggested that the deceased was at least seventy years old when he died.[5]

While not all cairns, or stacked rocks, are burials, some are. Cairns, or piles of stone, were sometimes used as way markers but it is impossible to tell if they mark a burial, or a trail, or a landmark. Like other manmade features on the landscape, cairns should never be disturbed or dismantled. The building of the road, the unintentional scattering of the sandstone cairn and unearthing of human bone, and the happenstance discovery on Iron Jaw Creek led to the archaeological investigation of the site.

The Split-Rock Burial

Some ten thousand years after the Anzick child's death and six hundred years after the death of the elderly man at Iron Jaw

Creek, a young man in his late twenties was buried in another rock overhang known today as Split-Rock Ridge in northeastern Montana. In 1964, cousins hiking around the Mahoney Ranch in Garfield County discovered bone protruding from the sandy crevice. Instead of leaving the items, the cousins dug around in the sandy soil and removed bones and artifacts. The rancher and others subsequently returned to collect remaining items. Decades later, Montana State University professor Dr. Les Davis examined the collection and realized its significance.

Carbon dating of the individual's third molar revealed that he was between twenty-seven and thirty-three years old when he died, and fixed his death at some twelve hundred years ago, during what archaeologists call the Avonlea, or Late Pre-Contact period. His bone structure is consistent with Northwestern Plains indigenous populations of the time. The items associated with the burial illustrate traditions kept by early people for thousands of years. Like the Anzick child, this person was buried with prize weapons and personal items to carry him into the afterlife.[6]

There was no red ochre covering the grave goods or the remains, but the location of the burial in a rock-ledge overhang and the finely crafted projectile points associated with it, suggest similarities with the much older Anzick child's burial. Among the artifacts was a slender mammal rib or long bone possibly used to pressure-flake stone tools, essential in sharpening arrow points. The long bone tool—whatever its use might have been—is very similar to the long objects found at the Anzick Site and supports the idea of burial with a toolkit. Perhaps the cache was the deceased's own handiwork, or perhaps it was made by a master craftsman among his people.

Items in the burial revealed more details. The fine arrow points were for use with a bow and arrow, not an atlatl, underscoring the gradual change in weapon technology that occurred with the extinction of large animals during the earlier Paleoindian period. The Archaic, or middle, period gradually saw this switch as the big game hunters of the last ice age gave way to foragers of plants and hunters of deer, antelope, and smaller mammals. Ornamental stone disc beads and drilled shells also found with the remains not only suggest this was a person of high standing, but also that his people had a wide trade network and must have traveled extensively. Twenty-one of the twenty-four arrow points were crafted of porcellanite—a hard, dense rock resembling porcelain—not found locally but rather in abundant outcrops miles away in Southeastern Montana. Some of the shells are local freshwater mussels, but nineteen shells are Pacific marine mollusks. One drilled shell bead is of the *Olivella* species, found in the gulfs of Mexico and California and in both Pacific and Atlantic oceans.[7]

The Hagen Burial Mound

In 1937, Oscar T. Lewis, a Glendive rancher and self-taught archaeologist, discovered a curious, circular grass-covered mound on a high bluff overlooking the Yellowstone River in Dawson County. The mound proved to be part of a six-hundred-year-old earthen village of the terminal Pre-Contact period likely established by early Crow Indians when they split from the Hidatsa and moved west from modern-day North Dakota.

The first excavations at the Hagen Site, which later earned distinction with National Historic Landmark status in 1964, were funded by the Depression-era New Deal Works Progress Administration (WPA) of the 1930s. Archaeological projects in Montana brought needed employment, putting crews to work excavating sites. The Hagen site includes the mound, an earthen lodge, and twenty cache pits. The number of artifacts and bones recovered, however, indicates that the settlement was probably much larger. The Hagen Site may be the key to a crucial turning point of a people in transition from farmers to bison hunters.[8]

The mound or raised platform, forty-five feet in diameter and level on top, formed a perfectly engineered circle. Apparently constructed all at the same time, it contained a large number of human bone fragments, mostly skulls, mandibles, and teeth. Dr. William Mulloy, who oversaw the excavations, concluded that it was a ceremonial complex. The skeletal remains represented many individuals. Some mandibles appeared violently disarticulated, or separated, with stone implements. Historically, the Mandan, Hidatsa, and other Northern Plains tribes buried their dead above ground on raised scaffolds. While some left the dead to return to the elements, others gathered the bones for burial. The Mandan retrieved the bodies after the tissue disintegrated. They separated and bundled the bones, burying the skeletal remains, and placed the skulls—with the mandibles aggressively disarticulated—in a mortuary circle. Mulloy believed the platform seemed to correspond to this Mandan practice.[9]

The Hagen Site National Historic Landmark is one of only two late pre-contact village sites excavated in Montana. People of this period and later in Montana did not typically live in permanent villages, make highly decorated pottery, or practice agriculture. Rather they lived a nomadic lifestyle as bison hunters. The Hagen Site's earthen lodge, however, suggests a permanent settlement and the ceremonial mound further suggests that it was a place of long occupancy. Agricultural implements, including bison-bone hoes and picks for planting, are among the thousands of artifacts recovered from the site. However, there is no direct evidence that these people were growing crops. Rather, the remains of three hundred forty bison suggest a hunting orientation and a lifestyle in flux.[10]

Remains at Pictograph Cave

Pictograph Cave, like the Hagen Site, was designated a National Historic Landmark in 1964, and like the Hagen Site, Oscar T. Lewis served as foreman of the first excavations in the 1930s. The site includes three caves near Billings that were occupied over a long time period spanning several thousand years. The site is exceptional for its continuous occupation; for the rare preservation of perishable items such as basketry, leather goods, and foodstuffs found in the caves; and for its art. More than one hundred pictographs (now mostly faded) are believed to represent events and eras from the early occupations through the acquisition of guns and horses in the 1750s and later.

The extraordinary art in the caves was known to Billings's early pioneers who claimed that when the caves were discovered, vessels containing red pigment—presumably ochre—used in the most recent paintings, were found intact in the caves. Nonetheless Sioux, Cheyenne, Crow, and Blackfeet claim no knowledge of the art in the caves. According to Sioux lore, one day a giant descended from above and sat on a cliff; the next day, the pictures filled the caves. Elder Crow in the 1920s did know of a battle between Sioux and Cheyenne and soldiers. This battle may be one of the scenes depicted on the cave walls.[11]

The oldest occupations, Late Paleoindian and Middle Archaic, in Pictograph and Ghost caves are poorly documented although artifacts of those periods are found in the collection.[12] The site serves as an important example of how early archaeological excavations—however well-intended—sometimes led to muddled information, jumbled sequences of occupation, and artifacts that went missing. The early excavations included the first professional recovery of human remains in Montana. But before radiocarbon dating and other technologies, skeletal remains were not considered particularly important to understanding chronology and typology.

The project was unconventional by today's professional standards. Field workers set up their camp and slept within the excavations in Ghost Cave. This encroachment on the delicate cave floor and walls was not the only shocking practice. Some crew members even defaced the cave walls with graffiti. And, unlike most excavations where visitors were discouraged, officials encouraged tourism and thousands trampled over the site during the first years.

Henry Melville Sayre, an English professor at the Montana School of Mines in Butte, had taken a few courses in archaeology. Sayre led the first excavations at Pictograph Cave. Under foreman Oscar T. Lewis, two of the three caves—Pictograph and Ghost caves—were excavated in 1937 and 1938 under the auspices of the WPA. Workers found the remains of nine individuals, all from the later period before Euro-American contact. The exact locations or positions of the remains, or associated artifacts, were neither noted nor published.

While Oscar Lewis is credited with significant contributions to Montana archaeology, scandal marked the brief career of Mel-

2. WPA excavations at Pictograph Cave yielded the first professional recovery of human remains. Oscar Lewis in right corner. Photograph by Tim Urbaniak. Courtesy of the Custer Gallatin National Forest, U.S. Forest Service.

ville Sayre. Locals claimed that both Sayre and Lewis told fantastic tales. Lewis wildly speculated in his notes that notched bone projectile points found in the caves came from Inuits in the Arctic. He figured that the Inuits harpooned buffalo that did not die but migrated south where they were eventually killed by the early inhabitants of the Yellowstone Valley. The two also claimed to have found evidence that early occupants practiced cannibalism. They backed up their story with the supposed discovery of a human skull with knife marks consistent with removal of the tongue and butchered human rib bones bearing human teeth marks. While Sayre's formal report to Governor Roy Ayers is considerably less flamboyant, he does mention that some items yielded evidence consistent with cannibalistic activity.

Billings author Glendolin Damon Wagner wrote about the 1937 excavations and the wildly speculative theories of Sayre and Lewis.[13] Her work is important because it is the only detailed account of the excavation aside from project reports. Wagner seized on the fantastic tales and painted a vivid picture of the finds in Pictograph Cave, but she also describes what workers found on the cave floor beneath eight feet of wind-and-water-eroded debris, before the artifacts and various levels became hopelessly jumbled.

Excavators, she wrote, found that the occupation level eight feet down revealed much about the lifeways of its inhabitants. Matted grasses, brought in from outside, covered the cave floor and likely provided comfortable places for sleeping. Charcoal, found in scattered places among the grasses, served as cooking stations and for warmth. Tools and weapons littered the area including a projectile point tied with sinew thongs and feathers, polishing stones, scrapers for curing hides, and a carved bone amulet. A thong necklace strung with Pacific seashells indicates a wide trade network or distant travel. A lack of beads and metal indicates an early time period before contact with Euro-Americans. The cave floor also yielded the remains that brought about the theory of cannibalism. A human skull and bones, crushed by a heavy object or weapon, and rib bones "bearing marks of human teeth" fueled this controversial theory. Wagner further wrote that these early people had developed survival skills such as cooking with fire and making weapons, but "they still ate human prey caught in battle."[14]

Melville Sayre soon left the project and died a few years later at the age of thirty-three. Professional archaeologist Dr. William Mulloy assumed supervision of the Pictograph Cave excavations in 1941. He quickly put these tales to rest and effectively ended any discussion of the human remains. Subsequently, several later studies focused on the skeletal pathology, but meaningful cultural studies without carefully recorded provenience are impossible.

Burial Laws and Repatriation

Burials reveal significant practices and beliefs that transcend generations. The desire to place the dead in strategic places, like rock overhangs and shelves or ledges offering panoramic views of the vast landscape, carries over to the present desire to locate cemeteries in beautiful settings or scatter ashes in places special to the deceased. From the dawn of time, objects accompanied the dead to serve as memorials and to guarantee a safe journey or a smooth transition to the afterlife. Belief in an afterlife is integral in the lives of these early people who walked the land so long ago. Such evidence today inspires reverence for these first Montanans and even feelings of kinship with those who have gone before.

Burials are a sensitive subject. Human remains should be reported to authorities and left alone. A burial in a remote place does not mean that it was intentionally abandoned. Rather, it was most likely placed there for a reason and deserves the same consideration as a grave in a formally planned cemetery. Many believe that exhumation causes a disruption in the journey of the dead. The individuals discussed here have taught us much, but whether a person lived a thousand years ago or yesterday, the dead deserve respect.

In 1986 when Northern Cheyenne leaders discovered that the Smithsonian Institution was warehousing some 18,500 human remains, mostly Native Americans, the federal government responded with legislation. The Native American Graves Protection and Repatriation Act, passed in 1990, was intended to rectify past abuses such as trafficking in grave goods and the disturbance of human remains. The law mandated the return of Native American "cultural items" to direct descendants, culturally affiliated Indian tribes, and Native Hawaiian organizations. This included human remains, funerary objects, sacred objects, and objects of cultural patrimony.

Montana followed thirty-five other states in 1991 with the passage of the Montana Human Skeletal Remains and Burial Site Protection Act. This act protects all burial sites regardless of cultural affiliation on both private and public lands. The act also created the Burial Preservation Board to protect all human skeletal remains, burial sites, and burial materials found on Montana's state and private lands, and to determine the validity of scientific study beyond identification. However, it failed to provide for previously discovered sites like the Anzick Site. In 2001, House Bill 165 expanded the 1991 act to include repatriation, empowering the Board to resolve claims for the return of human skeletal remains and funerary objects, and provided the exemption of Anzick lithic materials and nonhuman artifacts. This exemption allows much of the collection to remain on permanent display at the Montana Historical Society's museum.[15]

Following the intent of the law, on a rainy Saturday morning in June 2014, a small group gathered around a sealed concrete box holding the scant remains of the Anzick child. He gave the scientific community incredibly valuable information, but it was time for closure. Tribal elders and scientists came together for his reburial, a compromise between the potential for further knowledge and Native tradition. The Anzick child's potential to teach future scientists ended; those present at his reburial hoped his spirit could at last find peace.[16]

TWO

Mortuary Customs of the Upper Missouri Tribes

Sweeping Changes

Lewis and Clark's 1805–6 journeys across Montana are often interpreted as the dawn of the end of ancient lifeways and the opening of the West. The process, however, was already well underway. The eighteenth century brought the beginnings of sweeping changes to Montana's Native people and cultural practices stretching back thousands of years. Acquisition of horses and guns in the mid-1700s changed warfare and hunting methods and first contact with European traders and trappers made items previously unknown readily available. Iron pots, blankets, copper rings, trade beads, and myriad other items added new dimensions to the lives of Native peoples. These luxuries and conveniences came at a great price, for with them came alcohol and worse, epidemic diseases to which previously unexposed populations were exceedingly vulnerable.

Explorers, traders, trappers, and scholars recorded customs and cultural practices of the people they observed and knew well. They left fascinating observations about life and death among the Sioux, Crow, Blackfeet, Cheyenne, Assiniboine and Salish people. Mortuary customs and rituals may vary widely across the world's communities and even from tribe to tribe, but there are often similarities. Such traditions served, and continue to serve, universal and practical needs. Disposal of the body, the period of grieving, and the adjustment of those left to carry on were necessary concerns that assisted the living as well as honored the dead. Historical accounts reveal much about general beliefs and rituals, especially those describing death and its consequences. Many traditions and practices survived from great antiquity and some are practiced even today.

Common Mortuary Practices

Montana's tribes, like others across the North American Plains, usually interred their dead above ground in trees, on scaffolds, under rock piles, or on platforms in lodges. The dead were not usually grouped together but laid to rest singly in remote and isolated places. Montana's first people placed their dead in caves, on rock ledges, and in crevices like those described previously. But the various types of aboveground scaffold interments are very ancient as well. It was a common belief that that open-air interment allowed the spirit to travel freely and that belief persisted for thousands of years.

Edwin Thompson Denig (1812–58), an American Fur Company trader who rose to superintendent at Fort Union, had both Lakota and Assiniboine wives. Denig collected ethnographic information from various reliable sources, including scholars visiting the fort, other traders, and his own extended families. Writing in the mid-nineteenth century, he maintained that among the Assiniboine and others, scaffolding on trees was the most ancient and the most preferred method of interment. Death set in motion activities on several levels.

With the passing of an adult male, the body first had to be straightened and the face printed red. Those appointed to the task dressed the deceased in his finest regalia, wrapped a blanket around him and if the person was prominent, another layer of scarlet cloth completed the shroud. In ages past, painted skins served this purpose. Weapons and personal items placed next to the bundle included everything needed in the next life. A buffalo robe, wrapped skin side out and then tightly laced with strong cords, encased the entire assemblage. Strong men placed the bale in the fork of a suitable tree, away from predators, positioning the bale so the feet pointed down and the body faced south, looking to the South Wind where the spirit was to go. They tied the warrior's shield and other larger items separately to the branches. A lack of digging tools and frozen ground made earth burial less desirable, but occasionally a hilltop could suffice. The bale and the deceased's possessions were placed in the grave and heavy stones rolled onto the top to deter scavengers. Sometimes the assemblage was left in the open, covered with stones, dirt, and brush, much like the elderly man's grave at Iron Jaw Creek.[1]

After several days, mourners left the grave site unmarked and exposed to the elements. The Assiniboine followed an ancient custom placing a flag over the grave, especially if the deceased was a child. The fluttering scared away predators. But decay is inevitable and as the cords holding the bale slowly rotted away, it fell, or the winds blew it down. Birds, wolves, and other creatures of prey picked the bones clean. The family usually visited the site several times throughout the year. If the relatives found the bundle fallen and the bones scattered, non-relatives gathered and buried them. The family held another, less elaborate, secondary funeral during which a meal for those present was prepared and eaten and a portion left for the dead. But if the scaffold was intact, no one disturbed the dead. In the aftermath of grief, a female relative might receive a lock of the person's hair, wrapped around a piece of tobacco, to carry in a small bag in remembrance.[2]

Importance of Animals

In many cultures, it was customary to sacrifice animals or special pets to accompany the deceased to the afterlife. Many Indo-European cultures sacrificed horses for funerary purposes. Egyptians mummified horses, dogs and cats; Shang Dynasty Chinese buried dogs, sometimes alive, beneath the torso of the deceased. Mayans believed that dogs carried the body into the afterlife and thus dogs were often buried with loved ones. The idea of animals accompanying their owners to the afterlife is common practice among Montana's tribes but by no means unique.

Among the Blackfeet, Sioux, and others, it was customary to shoot the deceased's horse to carry him to the next life. If the deceased was a warrior, his favorite horse was groomed and painted

3. Horses accompanied their masters into the afterlife. H. F. Farny, *The Last Scene of the Last Act of the Sioux War*, 1891. Wood engraving. Library of Congress, LC-USZ62-133431.

with scenes of his master's prowess in war, the mane and tail braided and decorated with feathers, and then saddled with his owner's best tack. Leading the horse to the grave site, "a close relative of the dead man pressed the gun against the horse's head" and it was left where it fell to carry the dead on the final journey. If a person owned many horses, the sacrifice was even greater, and many horses might be left at the grave site. If the family could not afford to sacrifice the horse, they cut its mane and tail to show that the horse was also in mourning.[3]

Occasionally horses were sacrificed where a warrior fell. Artist Charles M. Russell tells how his beloved horse nearly met this fate. The horse, named Paint, was one of a herd captured from the Crow during a Blackfeet raid. One of the raiding warriors jumped on Paint's back as the herd stampeded. When the horses stopped running, the Blackfeet leader, Bad Wound, saw that one of his men was missing. He looked over the captive horses and noted blood on Paint's back. He wanted to send a good horse with the dead warrior on his last journey, and this horse that had

Customs of the Upper Missouri Tribes

carried him on his last ride was good and sound. So Bad Wound drew his Henry rifle, fired, and the horse fell. Bad Wound later saw this same horse among the herd with dried blood on his head and neck. The bullet had gone through his neck and the horse survived. But he was the steed of a dead man. No Blackfeet would ride a ghost horse and the horse was useless. Some months later, Bad Wound sold the "useless" horse to a young Charlie Russell. Renamed Monty, the horse lived to extreme old age.[4]

While horses gave their lives for warriors, dogs did the same for their female keepers. If the deceased was a woman, her possessions—sewing needles, cooking implements, and tools—were bundled with her. Her favorite dogs were killed and left to keep her company. Male or female—the funerary rituals were the same, but more or less elaborate depending on the person's social status. The mourning process required grief-stricken family members to cut their hair short and scarify, or cut, their legs. The Crow, Cheyenne, and Blackfeet cut off fingers as well, to leave at the grave site. Relatives mixed their blood with white clay, the symbol of mourning, and smeared it over their skin and clothing to be left untouched until it wore off. Close relatives, barefoot and scantily clad, remained near the grave for several days even in the coldest winter. Family members disposed of, or portioned out, the deceased's horses and possessions to strangers or to those who helped with the funerary rituals, depriving themselves of comforts such as blankets, skins, and even cooking pots. Sometimes there was fighting over these possessions, but propriety dictated that the family, in deep mourning, could not interfere. Smoking and feasting at the grave site were main rituals with food prepared for the mourners as well as for the spirit to take on its travels.[5]

Eyewitness Observances

Many variations of these rituals have been recorded by other observers. John Young, appointed Blackfeet agent in 1876, wrote similar accounts of scaffold interments, but he observed that if the deceased was a woman or a child, "it was thrown into the underbrush or jungle, where it soon became the prey of the wild ani-

---

mals." Such treatment in some cultures is not limited to women and children. Ancient Persians, according to seventeenth-century French author M. Pierre Muret, lay the dead in streets or fields hoping that animals would devour them. When the soul was consumed thus, encased in an animal's sturdy frame, it assured successful passage to the afterlife.[6]

Young asserted that the Blackfeet practiced neither cremation nor earth burial, and that his encounters with skeletons in trees and the "stench of half consumed remains in the brush" were very painful experiences. He further observed that women dressed the body and did the sewing up, "as the men would not touch nor remain in proximity to a dead body."[7]

Lieutenant James Bradley described a Sioux scaffold-type burial at the mouth of the Rosebud River in May of 1876. "Red-looking objects" on the riverbank caught his eye. Upon investigating, Bradley discovered "two Indian graves, the corpses being wrapped in red blankets and disposed in the customary manner on scaffolds, which had partly fallen down, leaving the bodies in a state of semi-suspension." Two scaffolds in the same place likely indicated some kinship between the two or a common date of death. He ordered one of the scaffolds dismantled to study Sioux burial practices and examine the articles placed with the body. The remains were those of a warrior who had probably been dead for about two years. Personal effects included a packet of letters and a soldier's hymn book. The letters, apparently from the soldier's wife, suggested that the soldier had been killed and his personal effects taken. In addition, there was a paper signed by Fanny Kelly with a note affirming her captivity. Bradley recalled that she had been taken from a wagon train in 1864 and held by the Sioux for five months before her ransom and return. Bradley speculated that this warrior had some part in her capture or captivity.[8]

Philetus W. Norris, the second superintendent of Yellowstone National Park, in 1876 observed the lodge burial of the Crow chief Long Horse. Buffalo hides sewn together and painted with horizontal brown and yellow alternating stripes and war scenes formed the walls of the thirty-foot high, oblong structure. Norris

4. Time has taken a toll on the lodge burials of two Blackfeet chiefs at Two Medicine Valley in Glacier National Park. Library of Congress, LC-USZ62-47820, Grantham Bain collection.

entered the lodge to find the deceased on a platform in a primitive open coffin. Long Horse lay in full war regalia, with scalps, weapons, and ornaments around him. An opening at the top of the lodge allowed ventilation and Norris noted that although the corpse had been there a month during hot weather, there was little offensive odor. "In fact," he noted, "I have seldom found much in a burial-teepee, and when this mode of burial is thus performed it is less repulsive."[9]

As in most cultures, mourning was, and is today, an important aspect of death for those left behind. African American trapper James Beckwourth, who was adopted into the Crow tribe and lived with them, carefully described scenes of mourning in 1834 after the death of the elderly A-Ra-Poo-Ash, chief of the River Crow:

> When we drew in sight of the village, we found every lodge laid prostrate. We entered amid shrieks, cries, and yells. Blood was streaming from every conceivable part of the bodies of all who were old enough to comprehend their loss. Hundreds of fingers

were dismembered; hair torn from the head lay in profusion about the paths, wails and moans in every direction assailed the ear, where unrestrained joy had a few hours before prevailed. This fearful mourning lasted until evening of the next day.[10]

Beckwourth claimed that thousands gathered to mourn the passing of the chief:

Such a scene of disorderly vociferous mourning no imagination can conceive nor any pen portray. Long Hair cut off a large roll of his hair, a thing he was never known to do before. The cutting and hacking of human flesh exceeded all my previous experience; fingers were dismembered as readily as twigs, and blood was poured out like water. Many of the warriors would cut two gashes nearly the entire length of their arm, then separating the skin from the flesh at one end, would grasp it in their other hand and rip it asunder to the shoulder. Others would carve various devices upon their breasts and shoulders and raise the skin in the same manner to make the scars show to advantage after the wound was healed. Some of their mutilations were ghastly and my heart sickened to look at them, but they would not appear to receive any pain from them.[11]

Changes in Customs Post Contact

After Euro-American contact and the arrival of traders who established posts, "box" interments—enclosing the body in a wooden coffin—became desirable to protect remains from predators. If a person died at a post or was near enough to be transported there, sometimes a coffin, large enough for the body and its attendant personal items, would be made. The "box" was then transported to a suitable location and elevated on a scaffold of poles or placed in a tree.[12]

The advent of Christian missionaries also prompted cultural changes. Repeated requests from the Bitterroot Salish for "black robes" brought Jesuit missionaries in 1841 to establish the first mission in the Northwest. St. Mary's in the Bitterroot Valley saw the conversion of many Salish to Catholicism. Native people who converted often adapted by taking some of the new beliefs and

5. Personal items placed on graves at the Sacred Heart Cemetery,
on Highway 2 near the Fort Belknap Reservation, comfort loved ones,
offer remembrance, and help the deceased transition
to the afterlife. Photograph by author.

combining them with their own older traditions. Missions, both
Catholic and Protestant, established burial grounds and encouraged converts to opt for burial in cemeteries. Not all Christian
converts followed these traditions, but at St. Mary's Mission, a
historic Salish cemetery dating to the 1860s lies adjacent to the
Catholic burial ground. Chief Victor was one of the first of his
people to accept Catholicism. He adapted to the new ways of
Christianity and built a proper house on the mission grounds.
When he died in 1870 while on a buffalo hunt near Three Forks,
his people carried him all the way back to St. Mary's for Christian burial.[13] The well-tended Salish burial ground, where Chief
Victor was laid to rest, sits with its unmarked graves in stark contrast to the adjacent tombstones and monuments of the Catholic cemetery.

Cultural interruptions such as the loss of tribal languages, out-
lawing traditional dances and celebrations, pressure to accept

Christianity, and the lack of written histories imposed monumental changes on traditional tribal cultures. Yet in the face of all these circumstances so devastating to Montana's first people, some cultural practices were so essential and the beliefs so significant that they carried over from the dim past, perhaps brought by those very first people across the Beringian Land Bridge and passed down over thousands of years to the clan of the Anzick child. Painting the face of the deceased red and wrapping the dead in red blankets thousands and thousands of years later substituted for the red ochre used by the earliest people. Burying needed items, a "toolkit," per se, with the deceased continued over time as well. An extension of the practice continues across many cultures in the modern custom of placing items on a loved one's grave.

THREE

Tragedy beyond Description

The Ravages of Smallpox

When Lewis and Clark and the Corps of Discovery maneuvered their pirogues across Montana's waterways in 1805, the first of the massive smallpox epidemics had already swept through the Upper Missouri country leaving a swath of death and disfigurement. White man's diseases—tuberculosis, diphtheria, measles, and whooping cough—eventually claimed many lives, but even these specters were not as widespread and terrifying as smallpox. The unrelenting monster caused the loss of thousands and thousands of lives among the tribes of the Upper Missouri.

So devastating was the first wave of the disease in 1780–81 that hundreds were left where they died and entire villages abandoned. Some years later, explorer David Thompson spent a winter with Saukamappee, an eighty-year-old Piegan Blackfeet, who survived the first epidemic and bore its disfiguring scars. He told Thompson that his people became sick when they raided an enemy band. It was nighttime when they stole into the village. As they slashed the lodges with sharp knives, they soon discovered that there was no one there to fight. All were dead and dying. The raiders carefully took the cleanest possessions of the dead, but smallpox followed them to their camp. Saukamappee said, "We had no belief that one man could give it to another, any more than a wounded man could give his wound to another."[1]

Smallpox, characterized by a high fever, chills, and ugly pustular blisters that cover the face and extremities, is a contagious, often fatal viral disease. In its milder form, two out of three patients recover, but each pock leaves a hideously disfiguring scar. In its more common, severe hemorrhagic form, the disease is nearly 100 percent fatal. Death comes swiftly from pneumonia, bone or skin infection, or in the worst cases, hemorrhaging from skin lesions and from the nose, mouth, and other areas of the body. There is no treatment. The last reported case in the United States was in 1949 and since the 1970s, the disease has been eradicated world-wide.

Europeans brought smallpox to the New World and to its indigenous people. There were numerous epidemics among European colonists and the disease eventually moved west. As smallpox ravaged Mexico and Texas in 1780, horses and the greater mobility they allowed likely helped spread the epidemic north. Known among the Indians as "many scabs" or "rotting face," smallpox crept into the lodges of diverse tribes. Although David Thompson was not an eyewitness, he was told that Chippewa and Sioux caught the disease around 1780 when they attacked white homesteaders afflicted with it, wore their clothing, and became sick. Thus, the spread of infection began. In the aftermath of this first terrible wave, wolves feasted on the hundreds of victims who died where they lay. Wolves that ate of the sick lost their hair, especially on their sides and bellies. For some six years afterwards, the pelts of those wolves were useless. Smallpox claimed so many lives that it caused severe cultural disruption and trade nearly ceased.[2]

1837–38 Epidemic

If the first smallpox epidemic diminished Native American populations in Montana, the epidemic of 1837–38 was "so appalling and so severe that for the succeeding decade traders, travelers, and officials all felt called upon to give accounts of its effects on the devastated tribes."[3] It began in June of 1837 when the steamship *St. Peter* (also spelled Peter's, Peters) carried the virus as it traveled from St. Louis up the Missouri River to Fort Clark near present-day Washburn, North Dakota. The disease spread quickly among the Mandan, Hidatsa and Arikara. The *St. Peter* moved on to Fort Union at the present-day North Dakota-Montana border. Two crew members had died on board and American Fur Company clerk Jacob Halsey was showing symptoms. Passengers and crew should have long been quarantined, but the cargo was unloaded and despite every effort to keep smallpox confined within the fort, it rapidly spread among the Assiniboine and others camped around the post.

Many residents of the fort were afflicted, and the fort closed to try to confine the disease. Jacob Halsey had been previously vaccinated and recovered but attempts to inoculate using Halsey's scabs proved fatal to some thirty people. Trader Charles Larpenteur, who was an eyewitness, wrote:

> there was such a stench in the fort that it could be smelt at the distance of 300 yards. It was awful—the scene in the fort, where some went crazy, and others were half eaten up by maggots before they died; yet, singular to say, not a single bad expression was ever uttered by a sick Indian. Many died, and those who recovered were so much disfigured that one could scarcely recognize them.[4]

Eyewitness and victim accounts are numerous and disturbing. One elderly Assiniboine, a youngster when he had the disease, recalled that as entire families lay dead and dying in their lodges, people came "and folded up the smoke flaps and barricaded the entrances. That served as their burial." He told of lying very ill in his lodge. His grandfather was near death and other family members lay dead around him. It must have seemed to outsiders that all in the lodge were already dead, and so someone sealed the smoke hole and blocked the entrance. Sometime later, the boy's sister came to grieve for her family and discovered that her brother still lived. She cared for him and he recovered to tell his story.[5]

A keelboat carrying trade goods and supplies from the *St. Peter* at Fort Union further spread the virus when it docked at Fort McKenzie, the main Piegan trade center. More than twenty-five died inside the fort. The first victims were buried, but so many died so quickly that grave digging was impossible, and the corrupt bodies were thrown into the river. Although warned of the danger, the Piegans awaiting trade goods had no concept of infectious disease and paid no heed. Several months went by and Alexander Culbertson, American Fur Company employee in charge of the fort, became concerned when no Indians came to trade. Culbertson was hardly recovered from a mild case but traveled to the Three Forks of the Missouri where the Piegans gathered:

> soon a stench was observed in the air . . . and presently the scene in all its horror was before them. . . . Hundreds of human beings, horses and dogs lay scattered everywhere among the lodges. . . . Some fled but the pestilence followed them seizing its victims on the prairie, in the valley, among the mountains, dotting the country with their corrupting bodies, till thousands had perished.[6]

Vaccination and Politics

Native Americans commonly believe that whites planted infected blankets to spread smallpox and annihilate Native populations. Most modern historians maintain that there is no evidence to substantiate that claim in the West. A single instance of possible intentional transmission may have occurred during the French and Indian War (1754–63) when the distribution of infected blankets was discussed at Fort Pitt, Pennsylvania. Whether or not the proposal was carried out is unknown. The theory of intentional spread among the Upper Missouri tribes makes little sense because most fur traders had Indian wives and partnered with the tribes. Further, there was no government presence in Montana at that time, and the intertwining of cultures was essential to maintain fur trading commerce. The belief that the *St. Peter* and others carried blankets intentionally infected has been perpetuated for so many generations that it is impossible to extirpate even though no evidence substantiates these claims.[7]

However, politics played a role in the devastation of the Upper Missouri tribes. Smallpox vaccination using matter from victims—as attempted at Fort Union—had been known for centuries. Edward Jenner's discovery in 1796 of a vaccine made from the sores of cattle infected with cowpox—a disease like smallpox but milder when contracted by humans—was a common, effec-

Tragedy beyond Description

tive practice by the 1830s. It was not, however, universal, even among whites.[8] Congress passed the Indian Vaccination Act of 1832 and appropriated funds to vaccinate Indians on the western frontier against smallpox. However, the act did not define "western frontier." This was a monumental effort, but it did not extend to the Blackfeet, Assiniboine, and other tribes caught in the 1837–38 epidemic. The exclusion was likely in part not only because government officials viewed the diminished fur trade as economically unimportant, but also because Secretary of War Lewis Cass viewed the Upper Missouri tribes as beyond the pale of civilization.[9]

At Fort McKenzie in the trade season after the epidemic, the American Fur Company purchased some ten thousand buffalo robes and sent them down river to the States. Many of these were most certainly taken from the hundreds of scattered, decomposing dead. Incredibly, there were neither reported outbreaks nor even a single example of smallpox from this unchecked distribution of infected goods. Mass infection annihilated whole tribes, but the "wholesale introduction . . . of robes taken from decomposing bodies" brought no harmful consequences.[10]

Records were not well kept and the numbers of actual casualties vary. We can never know for certain how many from any given tribe perished. But according to reports of the times, the Crow heeded the warnings having experienced near decimation in the 1780s and kept a distance. Still, a third of their number reportedly died. The Gros Ventres suffered fewer losses since some had been associated with tribes of the lower plains and been previously vaccinated. But half the Assiniboine and at least two thirds of the Blackfeet succumbed. The epidemic ended the Blackfeet's military supremacy, a force that was never regained: "It was a tragedy beyond description."[11]

Like the Black Death of fourteenth-century Europe that killed 60 percent of the population, the smallpox epidemics in the Northwest prevented the normal sequences of interment and mourning among Native populations. They also precipitated many suicides, of which there are numerous accounts. On one occasion near Fort Union, the favorite child of an Assiniboine named Little Dog died of the pestilence. Little Dog knew that the rest of the family would soon succumb and feared the horrible disfigurement that would cause them to appear disgusting in the afterlife. So Little Dog decided to kill the family before that happened. He told his wife of the plan and she agreed if Little Dog would kill her first, sparing her the grief of watching her children die. Little Dog agreed and carried out the plan, first killing all his horses and dogs. Then he killed his wife and finally cut the throats of his two remaining children before he killed himself.[12]

The last widespread smallpox epidemic in Montana occurred in 1869–70. In January 1870, during this epidemic, Colonel Eugene M. Baker and the U.S. Army took the lives of 173 unsuspecting Piegan Blackfeet. In the army's blundering quest for retaliation after the mid-1869 murder of trader Malcolm Clarke, Colonel Baker attacked the wrong village in below-zero weather, slaughtering men, women, and children. Soldiers burned the village and took one hundred forty women and children captive. When they discovered many of the captives were sick with smallpox, soldiers turned them loose in the bitter cold. As had happened so many times in the past century, in the spring the bleaching bones of victims dotted the prairies, and the coverings of abandoned lodges dismally flapped in the wind.[13]

Later Urban Smallpox Outbreaks

Cases of smallpox in Montana continued not only on the reservations but also among the general population through the later nineteenth and into the twentieth centuries. Fear of contagion of communicable diseases, especially smallpox, sometimes prompted communities to take extreme measures and even create impromptu burial grounds for the disposal of urban casualties. From April to September 1893, outbreaks of smallpox frightened Montanans in Great Falls, Helena, Missoula, and other towns. While epidemics were not usually given much press, smallpox was different because it was known to be highly contagious and unlike other communicable diseases of the time, vaccination was readily available. As today, not everyone trusted that precaution.

The situation in Anaconda and Butte was so serious that public health officials kept the press informed and urged all unvaccinated citizens to get vaccinated. Health officials set up "pest camps" in makeshift buildings and tents in isolated suburbs to care for patients in both Butte and Anaconda. Public fears were so intense that patients' belongings, household furnishings, and clothing were seized and burned and some public businesses, especially saloons, were ordered closed.

The epidemic cost Silver Bow County more than $8,000 ($235,280 in today's currency), not only in medical costs, but in replacement funds for citizens whose belongings were burned or businesses closed. County physician Dr. George W. Monroe applied for several months' lost wages claiming that he attended so many victims no one would patronize his private practice fearing the doctor was contagious. In January 1894, county statistics showed that there had been sixteen reported cases of smallpox in Silver Bow County in 1893 and three deaths.[14] Health laws dictated that those who died of smallpox be buried away from the general population with no relatives attending the interment. The burial locations of the three who succumbed are unknown, but interment was probably in the vicinity of the poor farm's pest camp and not in the poor farm cemetery itself.

Anaconda suffered more fatalities than Butte. A makeshift smallpox cemetery in a gulch southeast of the town once had rows of graves with white-washed wooden plank markers enclosed in a white-washed fence. At least six men and five-year-old Fay Slater, and likely others, who died in the nearby pest camp, were buried there. Convalescents usually dug the graves under the direction of the county physician, sometimes in the dark by lantern light. No trace of the fence, markers, or burial records remain to tell of the suffering that ended in the small, isolated plot of ground. The exact location has been lost to public memory.[15]

The Montana Legislature created the State Board of Health in 1901 partly because of the spread of smallpox and other communicable diseases. In that year, Butte, the largest population center, had 258 cases. Quarantine, vaccination, and better sanitation eventually controlled most outbreaks, greatly reducing mortality.

However, community smallpox epidemics continued. In 1905 an outbreak in Billings left eighteen people dead and 110 sickened. Schools closed and four mounted policemen enforced the quarantine of the sick. It was a common and dangerous practice to boil formaldehyde on kitchen stoves to disinfect the air. Some suffered serious lung damage. Again in 1907, Billings reported seventy cases. After January 1, 1910, the Montana State Board of Health discontinued quarantine but required confinement of victims. In 1919, on the heels of the Spanish influenza pandemic, Great Falls reported between twenty-five and thirty-five cases of smallpox.[16] Multiple, milder cases continued to surface in Montana until the 1940s.

The Aftermath

The crackdown on sanitation especially impacted the Native tradition of open-air burial. On the Fort Peck Reservation in the early 1900s, for example, the health department ordered the dismantling and burial of a group of scaffold interments. Helena dentist Dr. Eddy Crowley recalls that his grandmother, born in the 1890s, grew up on the Fort Peck Reservation. She remembered the scaffold interments and that the deceased were victims of smallpox. The scaffolds were taken down and the poles, belongings, and human remains buried in an open field. She and the other local children were sternly cautioned never to dig around or play in that field for fear of exhuming remains and spreading contagion.[17]

Loss of cultural traditions and the reasons behind them, however, especially impacted Native populations in the eighteenth and nineteenth centuries. Yet despite epidemics, wars, and governmental interference, traditional scaffold burials and associated rituals among Native American Montanans continued well into the twentieth century. Sanitation concerns ostensibly ended open-air interments, but many age-old customs survive to the present time, and even open-air burials in very remote places sometimes still occur. Some fundamental practices, like the use of red ochre and later, red blankets, survived from great antiquity. A close affinity with the natural world remains tantamount

Tragedy beyond Description

6. A collected skull and blanket-draped coffin sit on a fence surrounding an earthen grave on the Blackfeet reservation. Unidentified photographer, between 1880–1940. Montana Historical Society Photograph Archives.

in importance to today's tribal groups. They honor the deceased with songs, tobacco offerings, cutting the hair, and other rituals that have persisted through difficult times and many generations. Today's clergy are often willing to share funeral services with spiritual leaders and many funeral homes respect and will comply with the family's traditions.

Vaccination eventually ended smallpox in the United States, but the cataclysmic scars it left on many of Montana's Native populations can never be erased. A highway marker entitled In Memoriam along Route 2 on the Fort Peck Reservation is a poignant reminder that tribal groups still mourn ancestors lost to smallpox.

Epidemic Epilogue

Mass deaths and fear of contagion seriously interrupted normal mortuary practices among the general population historically and in the modern era as well. Smallpox, the Spanish influenza pandemic in 1918–20, and the current COVID-19 pandemic all brought about interruptions. Denying family access to the dying, prohibiting or restricting funerals, and limiting burial locations are some of the similarities among these community tragedies. Although victims of the Spanish Influenza pandemic were buried in established cemeteries, Montana law required that victims be buried within twenty-four hours of death, heads and faces had to be wrapped, caskets closed, and gatherings severely limited. Spanish flu infected an estimated five hundred million people globally and fifty million died. Five thousand Montanans, or 1 percent of the population, died of the Spanish flu.[18]

Severe restrictions for burials during COVID-19 include such warnings as not touching the body, carefully disinfecting possessions of the deceased, shortening funerals, holding virtual memorials or outside services at graveside with social distancing, and wearing masks. At this writing, the full impact of COVID-19 cannot be assessed, but it has disrupted lives and economies and brought death to many.

FOUR

Before There Was Billings

Place of the Skulls

Near the confluence of the Yellowstone River and Alkali Creek, which once flowed at the base of the bluffs in the center of modern-day Billings, there are several places where the landscape recalls thousands of years of occupation. Pictograph Cave, five miles south, is part of this greater tapestry, and so are the surrounding cliffs and bluffs that rise above the ancient creek bed. Some of these bluffs served as buffalo jumps, critical for the survival of generations of Native people. Stories associated with this important topography recall the aftermath of devastating events. While facts do not always match the numerous stories handed down in myriad versions, there is surviving physical evidence and oral histories that reinforce the importance of the area.

One of the historic features is a buffalo jump known as the Billings Bison Trap. Over many centuries, people used the Yellowstone Valley's plentiful natural resources and stampeded thundering herds of buffalo over the cliffs of the rocky escarpment. The rimrocks fall some four hundred feet to the valley floor where downtown Billings lies today. Hundreds of River Crow lodges once lay below in the shadow of the bluffs along Alkali Creek. It would have been a convenient campsite for butchering and processing buffalo for food, clothing, warm robes, and lodge coverings. Numerous similar versions of one story have been passed down, told by such Crow authorities as Plainfeather, Plenty Coups, and Henry Old Coyote. Crow Nation historian Joe Medicine Crow told it this way:

Two young warriors returning from a war expedition found their village stricken with smallpox. One discovered his sweetheart among the dying, and both warriors, grieving over loss of friends and family, were despondent and frustrated because nothing could alter the course of events. The young warriors dressed in their finest clothing and mounted a snow-white horse. Riding double and singing their death-songs, they drove the blindfolded horse over a cliff and landed at what is now the eastern end of the Yellowstone County Exhibition grounds. Six teenage boys and six teenage girls who were not afflicted with the disease witnessed the drama; they buried the dead warriors and left the camp.[1]

The bison trap area is known to local historians as "The Place Where the White Horse Went Down." Some versions claim the horse was gray or "pale," others say there were two horses, or there were many who rode to their deaths. Even the number of witnesses varies. Joe Medicine Crow's version above names twelve teenage witnesses, but in another telling of the story, he says there were fourteen teenage witnesses. Another version maintains that only one old woman lived to tell the tale.[2] Suicides were common during the epidemics, but the notion of sacrifice should have no role in the story. According to Henry Old Coyote, suicide was simply a last resort, an act of lost hope for a future. It was never an act to appease the gods as some have portrayed it. That is a modernization of the original event.[3]

In 1876, Lieutenant James Bradley passed through the Clark River Bottom where in the next year, the town of Coulson, and later, Billings, would be located. He noted petroglyphs carved into the face of one of the bluffs, slightly west of the present Metra Park. The Crow did not know who did the carving, but they knew the name of the bluff: "The Place of the Skulls." The River Crow had split into two groups with the smaller group—four thousand strong, according to Bradley's Crow guides—setting up camp along Alkali Creek at the base of the bluffs. The other group settled on the Powder River. An epidemic—probably smallpox—swept through the camp and bodies covered the area; horses and dogs

7. A freighter's outfit in the foreground includes a distant perspective of Coulson (right) which sits below the rimrocks north of the Yellowstone River where several tragic events took place. Unidentified photographer, 1882. Montana Historical Society Photograph Archives.

of the dead ran wild with no humans to care for them. The few survivors told the tale and later returned with others to collect the skulls scattered over the landscape. They placed them on a shelf that ran along the cliff face, about two-thirds of the way up.[4]

The Crow also told Bradley that two young men had stayed behind to care for the dying. They agreed that there was no future and leapt to their deaths off the cliff to the east of the Place of the Skulls. Bradley figured that the event had to have occurred no more than a century previous since the Crow had been in the area only about that long. This could coincide with the 1780 scourge or the 1837 epidemic or some other dire event. The Place of the Skulls is today called Skeleton Cliff. Slightly to the east of Skeleton Cliff, Boot Hill Cemetery (the burial ground of the early settlement of Coulson) lies on top of the Billings Bison Trap and the Place Where the White Horse Went Down.

Development has encroached, lowered the height of the cliff, and changed the view. Consequently, the bluff behind the Metra

8. The Face on the Rims is mortuary art that probably recalls
tragic events. Photograph by Tim Urbaniak.

Park does not appear high enough to have been the site of the
suicides. The rimrocks across the Yellowstone are more visually
dramatic and thus have been misidentified and misnamed "Sacrifice Cliff" on modern maps. According to Kevin Kooistra and
other locals, in the 1970s, someone decided that a change in
location to the much taller rimrocks across the river would better benefit tourism. So-called "Sacrifice Cliff" is on the opposite
side of the Yellowstone River south of I-90, not where the leap
supposedly occurred.

Faint, surviving art on the cliff face below the Place of the
Skulls depicts a crying, round face carved into the rock through
a layer of red ochre. The image, a combination petroglyph and
pictograph, is on the southeast side of Kelly Mountain, above
Sixth Avenue North looking over the Yellowstone River. One
historian suggests that the Place of the Skulls should translate
as "where the children are buried" although no source identified the skulls along the shelf as those of young people nor is
there any there reference to the deaths of children exclusively.
The Face on the Rims could be a motherly figure mourning for

Before There Was Billings

her people, her figurative children. It is unique among rock art in Montana but resembles at least one example in Washington State.

Tsagiglala, or "She Who Watches," at Horsethief Lake State Park near the Dalles, dates from about 1700 to 1840. It also combines pictograph and petroglyph art, overlooks a river—the Columbia—and is near a burial ground. Some believe that the circles around the eyes represent the sunken eyes of sick people. One theory is that the Montana image predates the Crow and is part of a mortuary ritual possibly linked to the death of a chief. The Crow or some other tribe may have adapted the image from their western travels. Whatever the origin, the crying image is generally accepted as mortuary art and further identifies the area as a place where tragic events occurred. The use of red ochre in creating the image follows cultural practices from the most distant antiquity.[5]

A Cemetery in the Trees

In 1877, a year after Lieutenant Bradley's visit to the area, the town of Coulson sprang forth below the bluffs. Dr. William Alonzo Allen, longtime Billings dentist, was working at the forge in his Coulson blacksmith shop. Across Alkali Creek, above the Place of the Skulls, a timbered outcrop kept catching his eye. Peculiar red streamers seemed to flutter over the trees. Upon investigating this oddity, Dr. Allen discovered a collection of tree interments. There were perhaps one hundred in all, in some cases two to a tree. The bales had begun to come apart as the cords weakened. The blanket shrouds unraveled and decayed; skeletons dangled, the bones rattling eerily in the wind. Possessions of the dead littered the ground: feathered head dresses, brass rings and beads, weapons and elk teeth that once adorned women's clothing. The cemetery of tree burials was long a place that settlers plundered, especially for the hundreds of elk teeth that were highly prized by the local fraternal Order of Elks.[6]

Mass burials like the tree interments above the Place of the Skulls are difficult to interpret and such a large group is unusual although during times of sickness, such groupings become necessary. The numerous oral histories that preserve the story of

9. Tree burials, like this Blackfeet interment, sometimes held more than one individual but rarely clustered in one area as in the cemetery on the rimrocks. Collected remains rest in the forks of the branches. Unidentified photographer, between 1890–1940. Montana Historical Society Photograph Archives.

the Place Where the White Horse Went Down—although they vary in some details—all agree that at some point in time there was an epidemic or some other event that claimed many lives. There is no indication that the burials were exclusively children. The crying face petroglyph and the stories substantiate the theory that the cemetery in the trees was—entirely or in part—the result of a dire event. Such out-of-the-norm mortuary practices can result from mass disasters, but such changes in behaviors are difficult to document.[7] When elders and tribal leaders die, community memory dims, and significant cultural identity can be lost.

The skulls on the shelf along the cliff that Bradley presumably saw in 1876 could have been gathered from the valley below following a catastrophic event. Some theorize that the skulls were retrieved from remains fallen from the tree scaffolds. The skulls would have eventually rolled downhill where Crow periodically collected them and laid them along the natural shelf.[8] In either case, their retrieval and placement for viewing certainly continues a cultural tradition long practiced, like the skulls and mandibles deposited over generations in the mound burials at the Hagen Site.

Immel and Jones

A skirmish in the rimrocks in 1823 adds another layer to the tragedies this prominent land feature, now in the heart of modern-day urban Billings, witnessed. On May 31, 1823, Blackfeet ambushed a group of twenty-nine Missouri Fur Company trappers led by Michael Immel and Robert Jones. Three to four hundred warriors waited until the party, riding single file, entered a narrow passage in the rimrocks. Armed with British rifles, the Indians descended upon the trappers. Immel, a physically powerful man who had a formidable reputation as an experienced mountain man, was at the head of the party. Immel was the first to die. So many bullets riddled his body that he was nearly cut in half. The trappers tried valiantly to fight, but there were too many attackers. Immel, Jones, and five others fell, and four trappers were wounded. Survivors buried the dead and escaped, but the company lost its horses, traps, and fine beaver pelts totaling $15,000.

The loss ruined the company. Joshua Pilcher, head of the Missouri Fur Company, removed his business from what would later become Montana. Benjamin O'Fallon, the U.S. American Indian Affairs agent, suspected that the rival British Hudson Bay Company instigated the trouble and had armed the attackers. The event had international implications and the stolen pelts did eventually end up in possession of the British rivals.[9]

The exact place of this massacre was long open to debate until Billings resident Harold Rixon pieced events together. South of Boot Hill Cemetery, at the eastern end of the north rimrocks where Sixth Avenue and Main Street come together, was once a landmark called Indian Rock. Mysterious petroglyphs—or pictographs as they are often referred to—seem to have depicted a battle, but they apparently were not of interest to early residents. During the 1880s after Billings was founded, clothier Joseph Zimmerman chose this prominent rock feature to advertise his business by painting a large sign over the images. Then in the early 1900s, workmen dynamited Indian Rock to make way for construction. The blast destroyed the rock and opened the crevice behind it that yielded the skulls of seven white men.[10]

Harold Rixon, a Berkeley college student at the time of the blast, later wrote in his notes:

> Roscoe F. Allen and I hiked to the Indian Rock to photo it, as we had aimed to do for years, and chalk over the pictographs so they would be clear in the photo. We arrived there about 3 p.m. and two men had just blown it up with dynamite. They had 7 skulls of whites. No beads, etc. Fragments of bones scattered all around, and [there was a] big pit in ground. The 7 skulls were in City Hall for months, but nobody could give any idea on it.[11]

It was not until 1953 when Fred Krieg, an expert on fur trade history, told Rixon the story of the Immel and Jones massacre. The pieces of the mystery of the skulls began to fit. The juncture of Main Street and Alkali Creek—the only place where the rims narrowed—matches cotemporary descriptions of the massacre site. It was the only Yellowstone River crossing.[12] The remains eventually disappeared, ending further examination. The killing of the Missouri Fur Company's key personnel impacted the fur trade in Montana for the next decades. Indian Rock, the massacre site, and the seven graves no longer exist. Now in the middle of urban Billings, the place where the rims narrowed was an important landmark that progress erased, and time has nearly forgotten.

FIVE

Conflict, Misfortune, and Uneasy Transitions

The Legacy of Progress

Fur trade, gold discoveries, and inevitable westward migration encroached upon cultures thousands of years in the making. Conflict and warfare left scars not only upon humans but also upon the landscape. Battlegrounds and massacre sites where conflict triggered casualties are unfortunately part of Montana's historic fabric and have left wounds that time can never completely heal. Such places of violent confrontation where blood stained the earth and the dead take eternal rest are a legacy of progress and change. Montana's historical landscapes contain some dramatic examples where the scars of human conflict and misfortune have altered its ambience.

Rapid changes generated tension among the varied players: between Native people and white newcomers, between the United States government and tribes, and even among whites themselves. Gold-hungry miners destroyed the pristine landscape, mining and homesteading encroached on Native lands, and the government pushed Montana's indigenous people onto reservations. Extreme changes in the latter half of the nineteenth century created opportunity for some and bloody conflict and misery for many.

Crimes and Death Among Newcomers

The gold rush attracted assorted humanity including well respected folks as well as unsavory types. Gold camps were full of people making new starts but also those wanting to cash in on others' good fortunes. It was good practice not to share too much information and keep private business private. The murders of Lloyd Magruder and four companions on a lonely trail in 1863 underscore the dangers of naivete, the greed the frenzied gold rushes fostered, and the criminal acts it provoked. These heinous murders helped trigger the vigilantism that characterizes Montana's first population boom.

Gold discoveries along Idaho's Salmon River and at Grasshopper Creek in Montana prompted Congress to create the vast territory of Idaho in 1863. The new territory encompassed present-day Idaho and Montana as well as much of Wyoming. The capital was at Lewiston, Idaho. The Southern Nez Perce Trail over the pass along the present-day Montana-Idaho border served miners, traders, and merchants as the most direct route from Elk City, Idaho, to the new gold fields and population centers at Bannack and Virginia City. Although a well-traveled pack trail, the route was dangerous not only for its extreme isolation and rugged terrain, but also because in that early period violence was common and law enforcement nearly non-existent. While there were ample opportunities to assess the character of a person in settled society, one took one's chances in the frontier West.[1]

After selling a load of goods in Virginia City, successful merchant Lloyd Magruder set out for home on this route in October of 1863. Magruder, a former candidate for Idaho Territory's congressional representative and a well-respected businessman, was traveling with four companions, some seventy pack mules laden with supplies, and $14,000 in gold dust. Four acquaintances from Virginia City joined the group. Magruder was unaware that these four men intended to steal his gold. As they camped just west of Nez Perce Pass, the criminals split Magruder's skull with an axe and killed his four companions. They rolled the mangled bodies in blankets and launched them over the side of a cliff into a deep gorge where they figured wolves could finish the remains. They burned the tack, threw metal items into the gorge, and turned dozens of pack animals loose.[2]

At daybreak, snow covered the grisly scene and the killers were certain no one could discover their crimes. But as they made their way along the trail, the pack mules they had turned loose began to follow the tinkling bell of the lead horse, as they had been trained to do. The criminals could not run them off and finally drove the dozens of mules into a canyon and slaughtered them.

When Magruder and his party failed to arrive, news spread throughout the territory fueling the fear and anger of an already nervous population. The disappearance of the large party and Magruder's popularity, coupled with other recent crimes, triggered outrage and helped push citizens to form the Montana vigilantes, organized at Nevada City in December of 1863.[3] Canteens full of gold dust and Magruder's horse stabled at Lewiston, Idaho, led to the capture and trial of the desperadoes. Three were tried, convicted, and hanged on March 4, 1864. The fourth testified against the other three. These were the first legal hangings in Idaho Territory. Magruder's friend Hill Beachy later discovered the gruesome remains, frozen at the bottom of the gorge, and buried what was left of the party in unmarked graves.

The remote ninety-five-mile route over Nez Perce Pass through three million acres of wilderness between Idaho and Montana is known today as the Magruder Road Corridor. It is the most treacherous, remote travel corridor in the United States. Breathtaking views remain unchanged, but for those who know its history, its spectacular beauty is a stark contrast to the ghastly fate that befell Magruder, his companions, and his pack train there.[4]

A period of vigilantism followed shortly on the heels of the ill-fated Magruder incident and other violent acts. Within weeks, vigilantes rounded up and hanged several dozen suspected criminals. The actions of the Montana vigilantes remain highly controversial and had far-reaching repercussions. Most of those whose lives ended at the end of the vigilantes' ropes lie in unmarked and unknown graves.

Virginia City and Bannack, both National Historic Landmarks, are the main places where the first Montana vigilantes did their work. These are the places, then, that are well-known to tourists for this earliest settlement period. But the lesser known, eerily remote Magruder Corridor preserves the unknown burial places of five unwitting victims of gold rush greed. The unpaved, lonely stretch deep in the Selway-Bitterroot Wilderness suggests the isolation and apprehension early travelers surely experienced.

The Thomas Tragedy

The endless procession of westward wagons and their occupants—over-eager for new beginnings in a new land—intruded on the homeland of previous generations. Newcomers' wanton killing of buffalo and wild game Indians depended upon for survival upset the harmony of thousands of years. The small, leather bound, penciled diary of William K. Thomas illustrates how retaliation was blunt and cruel.

William, his seven-year-old son, Charley, and driver Joseph Schultz left Illinois in May 1866. William had lost his wife and infant twin daughters to pneumonia, and he and Charley were headed to the Gallatin Valley to join his brother. William's diary describing his travels and feelings of forebodings is eerily prophetic. He recorded grisly details of the mutilated victims of Sioux retaliation he saw along the way. One common grave of five had been unearthed and the corpses eaten by wolves. At another grave site, predators had exposed the victim and gnawed his face; passersby could see that he had been scalped. William noted that "it was a sad sight to look at—but worse to reflect on."[5]

Traveling with a large train of other emigrants and freighters provided some safety, but they were intruding on Cheyenne and Sioux hunting grounds. Travelers had been warned of the danger. Once across the Big Horn River into Crow country, many assumed travel was safe since the Crow were peaceful. William, in his haste to get to his brother, broke from the train and traveled alone with Charley and Schultz for a week unmolested. Then on August 23, they camped upslope from the Yellowstone three miles east of present-day Greycliff.

Emigrants came upon the Thomas party's smoldering campfire the next day. Thirteen arrows pierced William's body; Charley's body had three; both had been scalped. The body of Schultz, half in the river where he had been fishing, carried a dozen arrows. Unusual marking sticks around the bodies of Charley and William—reeds tied with pods of cloth—may have held tobacco. What tribe committed the murders, Blackfeet or Sioux, has never been determined. Items salvaged and returned to the family included William's diary and one of Charley's well-worn, square-toed boots with a missing pull strap. Its mate was never found.

The three victims lie in a common grave off I-90 along the frontage road (old U.S. Route 10) between Greycliff and Reedpoint in Sweet Grass County. William's nephew, John Lienesch, located the grave site in 1937 and it was subsequently marked. Even with traffic whizzing by on the interstate, the site evokes a powerful message, recalling a violent moment in time and that our past is not too distant.[6]

Little Bighorn Battlefield

Montana unfortunately has star-crossed places where Native people and the U.S government clashed. Two such places of national significance are the Little Bighorn Battlefield National Monument in Big Horn County and the Big Hole National Battlefield Monument in Beaverhead County. In these two places, many lives were lost on both sides. There were so many casualties that each battlefield necessarily became a graveyard.

Indians defeated twelve companies of the Seventh Cavalry under Lieutenant Colonel George Armstrong Custer on June 25, 1876. Custer impetuously ordered his men to attack Indians camped along the Little Bighorn River. It took less than an hour for several thousand warriors to annihilate several hundred men. Major Marcus Reno and Captain Frederick Benteen's commands, fighting some distance away through that day and the next, survived. Although there have been various numbers of casualties reported, recent research suggests that more than 265 soldiers, more than thirty warriors, and ten women and children died.[7]

The American press immediately sensationalized the Battle of the Little Bighorn, or the Battle of the Greasy Grass (as the Bighorn River was known to the Lakota Sioux). It has become the obsession of students, scholars, and history buffs. Perhaps no other event has been so intensely studied and its minutiae both criticized and praised. It was a battle on a grand scale and for those who first came upon its aftermath, it was horrific.

To some, Custer was a brave and daring hero; to others, he was an impetuous, arrogant soldier who cared only for glory. Whatever the viewpoint, the battle was a pyrrhic victory for the Northern Cheyenne, Teton Sioux, and Arapaho who fought under chiefs Crazy Horse and Sitting Bull in resistance to life on government reservations. Lieutenant James Bradley, serving as commandant of the scouts accompanying General John Gibbon, was with the first men to come upon the battlefield, strewn with the bodies of men and horses, on June 27. The appalling scene revealed Custer's "entire command in the embrace of death."[8]

On June 28, 1876, in the aftermath of the battle, recovery of bodies began. The surviving Seventh Cavalry surveying the battlefield found unspeakable horrors. Three days in the sun left the bodies of men and horses bloated and black, the stench indescribable. Soldiers recovered and temporarily buried the remains of fallen officers, marking their shallow graves with the name written on a piece of paper rolled inside a spent cartridge. The cartridge, pounded into a wooden stake, provided identification. Privates' graves, however, were marked but without names.[9]

Most officers' bodies were later disinterred and sent to families or to Fort Leavenworth for burial although some, like that of Lieutenant J. J. Crittenden, remained buried on the battlefield at the family's request. Years later Crittenden's grave was moved to the nearby Custer National Cemetery. Lieutenant Colonel George Armstrong Custer was buried at West Point at his wife's request.

During the ensuing years, there were numerous attempts to gather the fallen. Wind and rain brought exposure of remains, and animals continued to carry off portions of exposed corpses. In 1881, after several burials and reburials, U.S. Second Cavalry soldiers under the direction of Lieutenant Charles F. Row, gathered all they could recover and placed the remains in a common trench. The soldiers' final monument was the common burial ground of privates and civilians and the result of years of hard work.

10. A soldier labels Lieutenant J. J. Crittenden's headboard at Calhoun's Hill on the Little Bighorn Battlefield. Library of Congress, LC-USZ62-51708. Photograph by Stanley J. Morrow, 1879.

The monument endures, set upon the crest of Last Stand Hill, close to where Custer himself reportedly fell. Nearby, rows of white marble headstones with no associated remains further commemorate the fallen. During work on the site in the 1980s, archaeologists recovered remains throughout the battlefield that have been reburied in the national cemetery as "Unknowns." It is unlikely that all human remains will ever be recovered.

Among the names on the monument of the fallen U.S. Seventh Cavalry is one that appears last on the list of the few civilian casualties, in the lower right corner. Isaiah Dorman was Custer's interpreter. Dorman had a Sioux wife, had lived with the Sioux, and knew the Lakota language very well. He took the job as interpreter at Custer's urging with the promise of higher than usual pay. He found himself amid this terrible conflict against his own adopted people. Dorman, born free in Pennsylvania, was the only African American to fall at Little Bighorn. A hero who lived an incredible life during times of discrimination and prejudice, the manner of Dorman's commemoration on the monument seems to belittle his sacrifice and underscore the racial boundaries that permeated even the western frontier. He is remembered on that monument by only his first name, "Isaiah."

Lieutenant Row also directed his men to dig a large grave for equine casualties. Soldiers typically shot their mounts and used them as defensive cover. The only surviving cavalry horse, not taken as spoils of war or put down because of injuries, was Captain Myles Keogh's Comanche. In their first inventory of casualties, the men of the Seventh found him badly wounded and nearly dead from loss of blood. The farrier led him fifteen miles back to the waiting steamer *Far West*, and eventually nursed him back to health. Comanche, however, never carried another man on his back and was a much-loved hero to the Seventh that symbolized the losses at Little Bighorn. By 1881, the bleached bones of dozens of fallen horses still littered the battlefield. The bones were gathered and buried. A marble headstone marks the Seventh Cavalry Horse Cemetery and acknowledges equine service.

After the soldiers' initial recovery of remains, Lieutenant Bradley wrote a letter to the *Helena Herald* contradicting rampant tales of widespread mutilations. Some soldiers had been scalped and their clothing taken, and some who had fallen near the Indian village had been horribly defiled by women and children, but that was not the case in most casualties. Tales that Custer's heart had been cut out were untrue. Although his clothing had been pillaged and he was naked, he lay unmolested. According to

11. Intermingled horse and human bones, photographed in 1877, a year after the battle, littered the Little Bighorn Battlefield. / Wikimedia Commons contributors, https://commons.wikimedia.org/w/index.php ?title=File:%22Scene_of_Gen._Custer%27s_last_stand,_looking_in_the _direction_of_the_ford_and_the_Indian_village.%22_A_pile_of_ bones_on_the_-_NARA_-_530869.tif&oldid=181773425.

Bradley, his wounds were not even obvious, and he appeared to be sleeping peacefully with no evidence of the horror of battle.[10]

There have been few changes to the terrain since 1876. The battlefield became a national park in 1940. The monument to the fallen men crowns the windswept hill while the National Cemetery, with its neat rows of white markers, stretches down a gentle slope. The five thousand graves are the resting places of soldiers and civilians—men, women, and children—who mostly died in Montana's remote outposts. The exact place where Custer fell is unknown although it is presumed to be somewhere within six feet of the monument. The Sioux, however, had a story about that.

A curious tidbit from the Deer Lodge *New North-west* of 1890 notes a legend supposedly told by Sioux who survived the battle. They claimed that on the hill where Custer fell, a peculiar plant grew. It had never been seen there before the battle and it is not known to grow anywhere else. Its broad, flat leaves curve like a sword, and its saber-like edges will slice through the skin like a razor blade. Those who unknowingly pick this plant drop it right away as its leaves are strangely cold and clammy. The plant bears a beautiful golden blossom with a center shaped like a heart. In this center there is one small spot of brilliant red, like a drop of blood. Indians called it Custer's Heart and refused to touch it, claiming that the blossom crushed in the hand left an indelible blood-red stain.[11]

Most recently, an Indian Memorial commemorates the tribes that also took a last stand, fighting to protect their families and preserve their way of life. Interpretation of the Indians' perspective was essentially overlooked until 1991 when the Park Service reimaged the battlefield and minimized the focus on Custer. Scaffold interment was the usual practice among tribes involved and there are no known Indian remains on the battlefield. However, early on, some twenty cairns were located indicating where some Indians fell.

Big Hole Battlefield

The Big Hole Battlefield National Monument represents one of the last and most dramatic engagements of Indian Wars in the American West. The nontreaty Nez Perce, pushed from their homelands in Washington, Oregon, and Idaho, refused to move to the reservation at Clearwater River, Idaho. After a skirmish in Idaho where five white settlers were killed, some eight hundred Nez Perce with several thousand head of livestock fled into Montana initially hoping to find sanctuary with the Crow in the

Yellowstone Valley. They had no quarrel with Montanans and doubted that General O. O Howard's army would pursue them across the Idaho line. They felt safe camping in the lush Big Hole Valley and intended to spend several days in peace. Eighty-nine lodges formed a V along the south side of the North Fork of the Big Hole River. On the north side, scrubby willows and sloughs stretched for a half mile to the pine-covered mountain slopes. The men organized a hunting party and the women busily peeled freshly cut pine poles for travois and tepees and dug ovens for roasting camas roots.

The Nez Perce posted no sentries on the night of August 8, 1877. They had no idea that Colonel John Gibbon and a small army of less than two hundred soldiers and local volunteers was creeping through the pine forest to surprise the sleeping camp at sunrise. Although the army claimed a substantial victory, the outcome was not so clear-cut. The Indians outmaneuvered the army, but the cost was crippling. The Nez Perce retreated without possessions, food, or shelter. Although casualty counts vary, the army counted twenty-nine dead and forty wounded. The Nez Perce lost eighty-three on the battlefield and others who later died of wounds. The majority were women and children.[12]

Many eyewitnesses document atrocities and carnage left on the battlefield. Human remains and the bloated bodies of horses lay scattered across the landscape in the hot August sun. Years afterward, participants continued to justify their actions. One volunteer, a Bitterroot Valley rancher, wrote in 1915 that the Nez Perce women were firing Winchesters as skillfully as the men and that the children were with their fighting parents, "violating the laws of our land; and we as soldiers, were ordered to fire and we did."[13]

On the morning of August 11, General O. O. Howard and his advance cavalry were first on the scene after the battle. They found most of the wounded in the rifle pits. Using newly issued experimental trowel bayonets as shovels, soldiers had frantically dug shallow depressions among the trees. Many later maintained that these experimental bayonets saved their lives.[14] Bringing ambulance wagons and tents, doctors and volunteer relief workers arrived from Helena, Deer Lodge, and Butte to help care for the dozens of wounded. Operating without ether or chloroform, Helena teamster Hugh Kirkendall held the patients down while doctors operated by light of a kerosene lantern long into the night. Dressing wounds while traveling was impossible and upon arrival at sisters' hospital in Deer Lodge, some of the men were "literally alive with maggots."[15]

Both sides returned to bury the dead, scattered over a mile and a half. Nez Perce interred some along the riverbanks, where the loose soil easily covered the bodies, and others in the shallow camas ovens. Soldiers buried their casualties where they fell, including Lieutenant James Bradley and Captain William Logan. Howard's Indian scouts had desecrated the remains of some; both Bradley and Logan had been scalped. The soldiers fashioned headboards—the term for shaped or carved wooden markers—out of pieces of wooden cracker boxes with name, company, and regiment, or town in the case of volunteers, carved or written upon them.

Many visited the battlefield in the ensuing weeks, reporting grim details. Surviving Nez Perce had fled in such haste that all the possessions of the dead and the living were left in tepees and scattered across the battlefield. One volunteer gathered thirty-two buffalo robes, some bloodstained, and sold them for good prices as relics of the battle.[16] Bears and other scavengers had unearthed the burials and feasted on the remains, scattering putrid corpses a second time.

Soldiers from Fort Missoula and volunteers returned on September 19 to rebury their dead. They gathered the remains of Bradley, Logan, and volunteer soldiers for reburial in local cemeteries, but other military casualties were reburied on the battlefield. It is unclear whether they were buried in a mass grave or individually. They did not attempt to reinter the dead Nez Perce.

In the several years following the battle, Granville Stuart and Andrew Garcia left vivid impressions of the aftermath. On May 11, 1878, Stuart visited the site and sketched the battlefield. He also sketched the grave of Private James McGuire with a pair of shoes and skeletal remains tumbled from the grave. Andrew Garcia and his wife, In-who-lise, visited the site two years after the event to find the grave of her sister. In-who-lise had been wounded in the battle and her sister killed. Garcia wrote:

> I hope to God I never see a sight like it again! . . . Human bones were scattered through the long grass and among the willows across the creek, and on this side of the creek human bones and leering skulls were scattered around as though they had never been buried. Still, it looked as if the soldiers had been buried where they fell and were in fair condition.

He further observed that peeled lodgepoles lay scattered, as undamaged as when the women laid them out to dry. He imagined their laughter, unaware that tomorrow they would be singing their death songs. The sight haunted him as did the eerie mourning cries of In-who-lise echoing across the beautiful, still valley.[17]

Author G. O. Shields walked the battlefield in the 1880s and wrote:

> the battle-field tells its own mute story even now. As I walked over it and saw the hundreds of bullet marks on trees, rocks, and logs I was impressed with the remarkable accuracy of the shooting done by the Indians. Nearly every tree and every object in the valley and in the mouth of Battle Gulch capable of bearing a bullet is cut and scarred in a frightful manner, and some of the trees are literally girdled. Many of the teepee poles that still lie scattered over the river bottom have bullet holes in them, and thousands of empty cartridge shells still lie scattered over the field.

Shields also noted that during the summers, neighboring ranchmen were still finding skeletons in wooded areas several miles from the battlefield where the mortally wounded had either been carried and hidden or escaped to die.[18]

Spoils of battle—like the buffalo robes—were not only taken by whites. Upon the death of Captain Logan, the little finger on his left hand was severed and two distinctive rings—a signet ring with the Logan family crest and a Masonic ring—taken from it. Logan's wife advertised in the papers to recover the heirlooms but had no luck. Several decades later, one ring was recovered from a trapper who had acquired it in trade. A few years later in 1900, Logan's son, then the Blackfeet agent at Browning, discov-

12. Granville Stuart visited the Big Hole Battlefield and noted scattered remains including bones and clothing at the grave of James McGuire. "Poor Fellow," Granville Stuart sketch, May 1878. Montana Historical Society Museum Collection.

ered the Masonic ring in possession of an Indian woman who had inherited it from her husband. Years before, her husband had severed the finger of a dead Nez Perce, killed in a battle with the Blackfeet and Piegans, and taken the ring. The two rings, returned to the Logan family, had come full circle.[19]

Big Hole National Battlefield is both an historic site and a monument. There are few encroachments; the valley appears very much as it did in 1877. Rifle pits dot the scrubby forest and a fenced military monument, placed in 1883, commemorates the soldiers who died. But climbing the trail to a sweeping overlook, skeletons of tepees are a much more poignant reminder of the families whose lives were cut short on that early August morning.

The Sad Tale of Head Chief

The buffalo were gone, game was scarce, and survival of the Northern Cheyenne on the reservation along the Tongue River in southeastern Montana depended upon government rations. Non-Indians ranched and homesteaded on reservation land and by 1890, food was scarce for the Northern Cheyenne. Starving families tried to exist on government rations, but soldiers took the choice items for themselves and it was hard to make the often rotten and wormy leftovers last until the next ration day. Conflicts arose when desperate Cheyenne occasionally poached ranchers' cattle.

Head Chief was an angry young man, the product of a long line of warriors, eager to prove himself in battle. But the days of warfare had passed, and he had no opportunity to accomplish this. Head Chief was courting a girl whose family was starving and so Head Chief, wanting to impress her, foolishly promised to bring her meat. He and his friend, John Young Mule, set off on a hunting trip but could find no game. Instead, Head Chief killed a rancher's cow. As Head Chief and Young Mule butchered the cow, Hugh Boyle, the rancher's teenage nephew, came upon the pair. During the altercation that ensued, Head Chief killed Boyle.[20]

When officials discovered the body, the Indians feared that whites would seek justice by attacking their camps. Realizing the violence that could erupt, Head Chief confessed to his people. He knew that the soldiers would hang him "like a dog," and he refused to give himself up. However, he promised, "I will play with the soldiers on ration day outside of town. I will die like a man." Head Chief 's friend, Young Mule, was not guilty, but he had no family and no one who cared about him, so he offered to ride with Head Chief. "Suicide by police" gave the two young men a chance to prove their bravery and die with honor.

A detachment of mounted troops and Indian police at Lame Deer in Rosebud County stood ready. It was ration day and many people crowded around, knowing that a tragedy was about to unfold. The crowd was tense, and soldiers rode among the bystanders warning them not to fire weapons or provoke action. Mounted on their horses, Head Chief and Young Mule waited at the top of Squaw Hill, as it was then called. They intended to ride the gauntlet, down the hill and through the line of armed soldiers.

The young men galloped down the hill as bullets whizzed. They made it past the soldiers, circled around, and started back up the hill. Head Chief reached the top, but a bullet disabled Young Mule's horse. Head Chief galloped down the hill a second time. Although wounded, he made it through the soldiers' firing line, then fell from his horse, and an officer shot him in the head. Meanwhile, Young Mule raced down the hill on foot. At first, he managed to dodge bullets and even returned fire. Then he dove into a hollow, trying to take cover, but there he was mortally wounded.[21] Bullet holes riddled the hill and the scars remained long after the tragedy.

The bodies of the two young men were carried to the crest of the hill near their death sites and covered in timber, according to custom. As years passed, the timber decayed exposing the bones. More than half a century later, few knew where to find the graves, but Head Chief's skull, with two bullet holes, was still visible to those who knew where to look. The hill is known today as Head Chief and Young Mule Hill.

In Summary

There is a vast difference between the ambience of cemeteries, where loved ones are carefully laid to eternal rest, and places where lives were lost during violent events. The latter places seem to capture and preserve the essence of the highest form of human angst. The onslaught of newcomers who fought among themselves destroyed pristine hunting grounds, wantonly killed and wasted game critical to survival, and disrupted ancient life-ways. The Magruder Corridor, the Thomas Massacre Site, Bighorn and Big Hole battlefields, and Head Chief and Young Mule Hill are public places where conflict became personal. These places illustrate the negative energies of the latter half of the nineteenth century on both sides of a profound transition.

SIX

Death in Montana's Early Communities

Rest in Anonymity

Migration west, for those brave enough to journey into the unknown, took courage and luck. No matter how well prepared, or how brave, or how strong the sojourner, things could always take a turn as the Thomas family discovered on the lonely cutoff to the Gallatin Valley. Others before them and after learned harsh lessons. Native people, missionaries, traders, miners, ranchers, merchants and homesteaders—the grim reaper was not selective. Montana's modern landscape is strewn with the resting places of thousands and thousands of those who came before. Their dust has blown across the prairies, their bones lie in mountain passes and niches, and their anonymous graves lie beside trails, along wagon roads, and in abandoned cemeteries.

Once settlers began to add their dead to the soil, early graves were haphazard. Sometimes rocks encircle these historic grave sites, or a simple triangle of three stones, or even a forked stick marks a burial, but most often early graves—even in urban cemeteries—were left unmarked:

> Some of the noblest men and women . . . lie buried there; yet their resting places cannot be identified. After considerable inquiry, we do not find that plot of the lots . . . is kept. The county gravedigger keeps no record of interments. He digs a hole and covers a corpse and the name of the dead is buried in the same oblivion as is his body.[1]

13. Montana's landscape is strewn with thousands of forgotten graves. Funerals, like that of a cowboy, were quick and life went on. Unidentified photographer, between 1885 and 1920. Montana Historical Society Photograph Archives.

Montana had no tombstone makers until the late 1870s and wood for headboards or homemade crosses was sometimes scarce. Ordering a proper headstone from the general store before the 1883 advent of the Northern Pacific Railway was cost prohibitive for most, given the expense of freighting such a heavy item by ox or mule train. Besides, it took months and the population was so transient that proper marking of a grave was often impractical.

Trading Post Cemeteries

Montana's first trading posts and forts were not defensive but rather intended for commerce. These early communities established the first earthen burial grounds. Two of Montana's trading posts, Fort Connah in the Flathead region of Lake County and Fort Benton at the head of navigation on the Missouri River in Chouteau County, illustrate how burial grounds were sometimes revered and sometimes necessarily lost. Both forts date to the 1840s. Cemetery preservation or obliteration usually depends heavily upon two factors: continued relationships of the living with those interred and the need for progress. Location also plays a major role as these two cemeteries demonstrate.

Fort Connen, originally named for a river in Scotland, became known as Fort Connah through Native American usage. Hudson's Bay Company, the British rival of American companies, founded the fort near present-day Arlee, in Lake County, in 1846. Although the Oregon Treaty had just established U.S. ownership of land below the 49th parallel, the fort long evaded the law and operated into the twilight of the fur trade because it dealt in hard-to-obtain items such as buffalo meat, buffalo skin saddle blankets, rawhide, and hair cordage. Scottish-born Angus MacDonald (also spelled McDonald) took charge of the fort in 1847 and later, his son Duncan—who was born at the fort—served as the last factor from circa 1868 until the post closed in 1871 due to encroaching settlement. The single surviving fort structure, completed in 1847 and listed in the National Register, is arguably Montana's oldest standing building.

Angus MacDonald died in 1889 and his wife Catherine, a Métis of Scotch, Iroquois, and Nez Perce blood, died in 1902. The small post cemetery, half a mile from the fort, holds MacDonald family members and a few others, and probably includes some earlier graves that are unmarked. The cemetery is still active with one family member buried there as recently as 2003. The tiny cemetery, half a mile from the fort, has been fortunately preserved and is maintained by local MacDonald descendants and the Fort Connah Restoration Society.

Fort Benton, a National Historic Landmark, was established as a trading post in 1847. It claims to be the birthplace of Montana, the state's oldest continuously occupied community. While most towns in the West grew decades later to serve mining, the railroad, or agriculture, Fort Benton was the last port along the Upper Missouri River and thus so strategically placed that it became the hub for both the import of goods and export of furs, buffalo robes and later, gold. In its first season in 1847, twenty thousand buffalo robes went downriver to St. Louis.[2] Contemporary with Fort Connah, Fort Benton was the American Fur Company's last Blackfeet trading post. At any given time, the population included many Native lodges with families camped around the fort.

Early Fort Benton was typical of other forts and most certainly had a cemetery where Native Americans, Métis of mixed Euro-American and Native ancestry, and post employees and their families could be properly buried. However, as Fort Benton quickly grew into a bustling port, the town grew up around it, and the post cemetery was forgotten. As the seat of Chouteau County, the county cemetery at Fort Benton was founded there in 1868. The settlement continued to grow until that cemetery was too close to town. Graves were moved to the current Riverside Cemetery in the early 1880s. No trace of either post cemetery or county cemetery survives. Riverside includes various sections for Catholics, protestants of various denominations, and fraternal organizations. Unmarked graves cannot today be identified. Fire in the Chouteau County courthouse destroyed records and removal of markers in the poor farm section outside the cemetery proper caused further loss of identities.[3]

Fort Benton's early identified remains—that is, those few marked with tombstones or headboards moved from the county cemetery—underscore the hazards of life in the nineteenth century. The Preston family, for example, lost two children to pneumonia in 1878 and a third in 1881. Weeks later, their father, William Preston, died suddenly leaving a wife and two remaining children. In 1876, teamster Edward Livingston was run over by a freight wagon and crushed to death; in 1872, Dennis Hinchey was shot four times and killed in a saloon. In 1879, Mrs. Margaret Morton and her eight-year-old daughter drowned crossing the Belt River in a wagon. A few months later, her husband, Michael Morton, having been acquitted of blame in the accident, became intoxicated and froze to death. These deaths and so many others convey the fact that life could end with cruel abruptness.[4]

Loss of early cemeteries like the two in Fort Benton are typical of early Montana communities. It is common to lose the locations of these earliest burial grounds unless family or the property owner oversees their maintenance. Hell Gate, the early community that moved to Missoula in 1865, is another example. It had some forty burials but urban development and changing landscape obliterated that location and it is unknown today. Demersville's cemetery, on the other hand, has survived even though the entire community and many of its buildings moved to the townsite of Kalispell circa 1892. And Frenchtown's St. John the Baptist Cemetery, established in 1864 and sited far enough from encroaching development, has also survived. The Demersville and Frenchtown cemeteries, typical of early communities, include an unknown number of unmarked burials.

Mission Cemeteries

St. Mary's Mission at present-day Stevensville in Ravalli County and Fort Benton were contemporary with each other. These two comprise Montana's first real communities; which one came first is a matter of semantics. Fort Benton was continuously inhabited from 1847, but Jesuits founded St. Mary's Mission—known as the "cradle of Montana"—in 1841. St. Mary's, founded in the Bitterroot Valley in the shadow of what the Jesuits named St. Mary's Peak, was the first of many Catholic missions in the Northwest. Jesuits there established Montana's first Catholic cemetery where newly converted Indians were buried. In 1845, Father Pietro Zerbinatti became the first priest to die in Montana. He was bathing in the nearby river when a cramp apparently overtook him, and he drowned. With many in attendance at his funeral, Father Zerbinatti was "laid to rest among the Indians."[5]

The mission closed in 1850 causing a lapse in habitation although John Owen purchased the property and founded Fort Owen nearby. The mission reopened in 1866 but in a different location. The original 1841 mission site and its burial grounds are today unknown. However, before knowledge of the first site was lost, Indians who had been present at Zerbinatti's funeral claimed to know where he was buried. In 1866, they directed the Jesuits in the disinterment of Zerbinatti's supposed remains, but there was some doubt about the identity. Jesuits took the bones to St. Ignatius Mission on the Flathead Indian Reservation where they lay forgotten in a corner of the sacristy. Father Lawrence B. Palladino retrieved them in 1884 and buried them in the St. Ignatius Mission Cemetery.[6]

14. Individual graves in the Salish cemetery at St. Mary's Mission
in Stevensville are unmarked. Photograph by author.

The second St. Mary's Mission Cemetery, established in 1866
and included in the National Register–listed St. Mary's Mission
Historic District, lies adjacent to the mission grounds. Its headstones reflect the various time periods and styles from the 1860s
to the present. The nearby Salish cemetery, also included in the
Register-listed district, stands in sharp contrast.

All burials there are unmarked. A modern granite marker
records the names of those known to be interred there. In the
center of the smooth, well-tended grounds, another marker reads
simply: "In prayerful remembrance of the brave hearts sleeping
in the shadow of St. Mary's."

The cemetery at St. Ignatius in present-day Lake County predates the current cemetery at St. Mary's. Father Pierre-Jean De
Smet established St. Ignatius Mission and its cemetery in 1854.
By 1855, at least a thousand Salish, Kootenai, Kalispell, and Pend
d' Oreille had settled around the mission. The mission cemetery quickly became overcrowded. Enlarged in the 1880s, it was

the final resting place for Jesuit priests, Sisters of Providence, and Ursuline Sisters, along with First Nation Catholic converts on the Flathead Indian Reservation. When a new parish cemetery opened at the town's southeast corner, the mission cemetery closed, and many burials were moved to the new site. Unfortunately, there is no comprehensive record of those moved. A few scattered headstones remain in the two square blocks of the old cemetery to at least mark the site where hundreds, and perhaps thousands, still lie beneath the sod. It remains a sacred place to the St. Ignatius community and it is Montana's oldest existing Catholic cemetery.

Catholic mission cemeteries, some active like that at St. Labre at Ashland in Rosebud County and others abandoned like St. Peter's Mission in Cascade County, are scattered across Montana.

Military Posts

The U.S. Army established Fort Shaw in 1867 in the Sun River Valley of Cascade County. The purpose of the outpost, in the heart of the Blackfeet Indian Nation, was to protect travelers along the Mullan Road between Fort Benton and Helena. Fort Shaw, listed in the National Register, was Montana Territory's first government presence and like all western outposts, it had its own cemetery for soldiers and civilians where some two hundred people were buried. Active until 1891, the fort then served as the government-run Fort Shaw Indian Industrial School for Indian children from 1892 to 1910. As many as two thousand children, many taken from their families and stripped of their cultural identities, lived at the school during that time period.

In 1894 the government began an effort to disinter and move those buried in fast-closing western forts. Seventy-four individuals buried at Fort Shaw were reinterred at the Custer National Cemetery on the Little Bighorn Battlefield site. The Fort Shaw cemetery continued in use, however, and thirty-three Indian students and others were buried there. The children died of diseases and epidemics, many of them in 1908 when whooping cough swept through the school. Deaths and burials were not confined to students at the fort. Within a week, school watchman J. H. McKnight lost three of his own six children, ages seven, nine, and three months, to that epidemic.[7]

Other Montana forts with identified burial grounds include short-lived Fort Logan, founded in 1870 near White Sulphur Springs in Meagher County. It served until 1880. The eight recorded burials in the Fort Logan cemetery, including military and civilians, were moved to Custer National Cemetery. National Register–listed Fort Keogh at Miles City, founded in 1877 in the aftermath of the Little Bighorn battle, became a government remount station in 1900, training and shipping horses for the military through World War I. Its cemetery includes only one identified burial and probably other unknowns.

The Fort Missoula Post Cemetery in the National Register–listed Fort Missoula Historic District at Missoula in Missoula County is an active Class IV National Military Cemetery administered by the U.S. Army. Surrounded by an iron fence, it has four hundred grave sites within its one acre. The fort dates to 1877 and includes veterans of many wars, African American buffalo soldiers stationed at the fort, and civilians. The cemetery is closed to new reservations.

Fort Harrison at Helena was founded in 1892 to help consolidate troops from smaller Montana forts. During World War II, the fort trained the army's First Special Service Force, and the fort today includes houses National Guard Joint Forces, an Army Reserve training center, and a Veterans Affairs hospital. The old post cemetery was located on the grounds of the present firing range. The first burial occurred in 1896. Forty graves were removed in 1948 and most reinterred in the Custer National Cemetery. At least one however, was moved to Helena's Forestvale Cemetery. Samuel Bridgewater, a buffalo soldier who served as cook at the fort, was wounded in the Spanish American War and died of related health problems in 1912. At the request of his family, Bridgewater was reinterred in the family plot at Forestvale.[8]

"Boot Hills" at Bannack, Nevada City, and Virginia City

While the Catholic church and its missions sometimes kept records of Catholic deaths and burials, reliable documentation is problematic for most communities until the twentieth century. This is especially the case during the chaotic 1860s before the advent of newspapers. But even then, the *Montana Post*—Montana's first newspaper founded in August 1864—did not always publish obituaries, death notices, or causes of death. Into the twentieth century, in fact, epidemics were poorly covered in the press for fear of causing panic, and death certificates were not required in Montana until 1908. However, there are some physical reminders of those who died violently "with their boots on" and others who died too soon in Montana's mining camps and boomtowns.

Discovery of gold touched off the first population booms in western Montana. The rush was a lottery: a few struck it rich, but most drew blanks. Violence—murders, robberies, and vigilante hangings—are significant to this early history. Every mining camp left a burial ground, most often located upon the community's highest vantage point. Some of these "boot hill" cemeteries survive to help tell the stories of those who died of violent causes or simply drew unlucky tickets.

Primitive mining camps posed serious health risks. Miners were notoriously careless with their water sources and streams became quickly polluted with mining by-products and human waste, breeding typhoid and cholera. If there were better records, the losses suffered in these early Montana communities would be surprising. And there were other dangers too. Gold rush doctors faced a battleground where stabbings, shootings, mining accidents, and frostbite added to the usual maladies and disasters affecting the population.

Children were especially vulnerable. In the nineteenth century, global statistics claim that one in every three children born died before the age of five. Dirty, crude log cabins and otherwise unsanitary living conditions were particularly unhealthy for children. Contagion was little understood and childhood diseases including whooping cough, scarlet fever, diphtheria, and measles were constant specters in the nineteenth-century West. Rocky Mountain spotted fever or "black measles," and mountain fever—a mysterious malady that affected newcomers of all ages—took serious tolls.

15. An early overview of Bannack includes Boot Hill, visible above the town in the center of the photograph. Unidentified photographer, between 1870–1900. Montana Historical Society Photograph Archives.

The locations of mining camp cemeteries where graves were frequently unmarked easily fell victim as residents moved on, buildings crumbled, time passed, and property owners developed or cultivated the land. Bannack, Nevada City, and Virginia City, however, fortunately retain their first burial grounds partly because those communities initially supported significant populations that were highly transient, and the areas remained rural and undeveloped without significant urban encroachment.

Gold discovered along Grasshopper Creek in 1862 gave birth to Bannack, Montana's first substantial gold rush boomtown and today a National Historic Landmark. "Boot Hill" was Bannack's first cemetery. Like most early Montana burial grounds, it was located on high ground. Nestled to the north upon a hilltop overlooking the town, it may be the state's earliest surviving community burial ground. It has one of Montana's oldest tombstones. Hand cut and crude, the stone marks the grave of William H.

16. Bannack moved its cemetery to more accessible lower ground around 1880. Photograph by author.

Bell, whose well-documented funeral was the first of its kind in Montana. As Bell lay dying of mountain fever, he requested a Masonic funeral. No one knew how many Masons might be in the gold camp. The summons went out and seventy-six Masons attended the funeral; William Bell was the seventy-seventh.[9]

Many of Bannack's first casualties rest in unmarked graves. Among them are victims of the vigilantes: Peter Horan, hanged in 1863; Buck Stinson and J. C. Rawley, hanged in 1864; and Joe Pizanthia, shot in 1864. Marked graves include that of sixteen-year-old Delia Cutler who died of unknown causes in 1865. The large imported, shared tombstone of Henry Trask, who died in a mining accident in 1865, and Charles Trask, who died in 1870, was added sometime after 1870. Difficult accessibility and the desire for a more formal burial ground is likely why the community established a new cemetery on lower ground around 1880.

Nevada City and Virginia City were sister communities that burgeoned with the discovery of gold at Alder Gulch in May of 1863. Nine gold camps straggled along the fourteen-mile gulch, but Virginia and Nevada were the largest and vied with each other. Each has its own history and early cemetery. Nevada City's cemetery has dozens of early unmarked burials including that of George Ives.[10] The trial and hanging of Ives in December 1863 was one of the most dramatic events in Montana's violent, early settlement history. Ives, accused of the brutal murder of Nicholas Tbalt (variously spelled Tbolt, Tiebolt), was tried and convicted on Nevada City's main street. The hanging took place soon after on the beam of an unfinished cabin and this event was the catalyst for the forming of the Montana vigilantes. Ives's grave was summarily unmarked and was among the first in the Nevada City Cemetery. According to legend, Tbalt was also interred there, his grave marked with a forked stick. The locations of these two graves are today unknown. Nevada City's cemetery survived because urban development never encroached, and generations of local ranching families have continued to bury loved ones there.

Virginia City's Boot Hill, included in the Virginia City National Historic Landmark, is one of the town's major attractions although this was not always the case. Into the early twentieth century, the exact burial places of the five accused road agents hanged in January 1864 were unknown to most residents. The five men—Haze Lyons, Jack Gallagher, Fred Parrish, Boone Helm, and "Clubfoot" George Lane—died almost simultaneously on the crossbeam of an unfinished building. The Hangman's Building survives today on Virginia City's Wallace Street. The five men were buried on the hill overlooking Virginia City. Three stones forming a triangle, a common way to delineate interments in lieu of formal headboards or tombstones, marked each grave. Others also buried on Boot Hill were similarly marked.[11] The stigma of lying forever near the five road agents was repugnant to many, prompting the establishment of a second cemetery.[12] Some residents who had loved ones buried on Boot Hill disinterred their remains and moved them to the newly opened Hillside Cemetery, also on high ground, just across the rise. Not all those buried on Boot Hill, however, had loved ones to accomplish such a task.

William and Clara Dalton were among those left to eternally repose on Boot Hill. The Daltons had come west on the first Fisk train in 1862 with their four teenage children. The family moved from Bannack to Virginia City in late 1863 where a typhoid epidemic, likely due to contaminated water, was taking a toll.[13] Daughter Mathilda came down with "the fever" while nursing four-year-old Lee Short who died. Mrs. Dalton fell ill caring for Mathilda and died. William succumbéd soon after; Matilda survived. Mathilda soon married Zebulon Thibadeau and she and her siblings moved on leaving their parents in unmarked graves on Boot Hill.[14]

According to Lew Calloway's firsthand account, two lines of undisturbed burials remained on Boot Hill in 1907, one line on top of the hill and another slightly downslope to the west. Controversy over which line contained the road agents' graves was settled when Callaway, Virginia City Mayor James G. Walker, Adriel B. Davis, and a few diggers assembled on the hill. Mayor Walker was also the current clerk of the court and thus had the power to authorize the project. Davis had been an active vigilante, had helped bury the five men, and knew the order of the burials. He pointed out the grave of George Lane. Lane's congenital foot deformity would confirm his identity and thus the graves of the others. Removing the sod overlay, about four feet down diggers encountered wooden boards that had been placed across a shelf on either side of the grave. Beneath the boards, the body had been wrapped in a blanket. Red drawers and a gray sock came to light. The deformed foot was removed and the mission accomplished. The shellacked foot, with a sock still attached, reposed for decades under glass on display in the Madison County courthouse and later at the local Thompson Hickman Museum.[15]

Many years later, the Daltons' grandchildren returned to Virginia City to place a commemorative monument on Boot Hill. This memorial stone, likely not on the actual burial plots, which are not known, and the five wooden markers on the road agents' graves, are the only indications that there are burials on Boot Hill. Although some may believe the road agents are not buried there, no documentation or local speculation whatsoever suggests otherwise. Chinese resident Ah Tong, who died in October 1865; Martin Lyon, murdered in January 1865; the Daltons; and other unknowns most certainly rest there as well.[16]

17. Dr. Jabez Robinson's aboveground crypt in Virginia City's Hillside Cemetery may not actually hold his remains. Photograph by Larry Goldsmith.

In 2016, distant relatives of George Lane reclaimed his foot from the Thompson Hickman Museum under the Native American Graves Protection and Repatriation Act. The foot was cremated, and family scattered the ashes over his grave. However, the museum had a replica made that is still on display.[17]

Hillside Cemetery, Virginia City's "new" burial ground, is one of Montana's oldest active cemeteries. Opened in 1866, its first interments marked with tombstones include *Montana Post* editor Thomas Dimsdale and Dr. Jabez Robinson; both died in 1866. Dr. Robinson's grave is of some interest. His grave site appears to be an aboveground brick burial vault, but according to his obituary, he is not buried there.

Dr. Robinson drowned attempting to cross a swollen stream when he was swept off his horse. His body was not recovered. Dr. Robinson, while an excellent physician, may not have been a popular man. His obituary in a Kansas newspaper described him as a "rabid" secessionist who fled to "Rebel Paradise, Montana." The article states in no uncertain terms that his fate was well deserved and perhaps there was little effort to recover his remains.[18] He left a wife who apparently erected a noble grave site for her husband, whether his body lies there or not.

Last Chance

Montana Territory was little more than six weeks old when gold, discovered in July 1864 at Last Chance, touched off Montana's third great gold rush. Miners, merchants, and service providers trickled in and by the end of October, some two hundred hearty souls had settled in the gulch, newly christened Helena. Much of the early population moved from Bannack to Virginia City and finally to Helena where, as elsewhere in the 1860s, vigilantes did their grisly work. Unlike most places, however, Helena had a hanging tree that served its gruesome purpose at least ten times and possibly more. Some of these hangings were carried out by the miners' court and some were lynchings. Some of the victims were reportedly buried in the city or Catholic cemeteries, but the burials of others went unrecorded. Some were most likely buried in a makeshift "boot hill" near the place of execution. Evidence has twice surfaced in what is now a residential neighborhood where the tree, cut down in 1875, once stood.

In 1900, workmen digging a foundation for an addition on a Highland Street home uncovered a skeleton. While the remains were initially identified as John Keene, sentenced by the miner's court for the murder of Harry Slater and hanged in 1865, that conclusion has been disputed.[19] A second set of remains surfaced in 1931 when workmen were installing gas lines in Davis Street. In this case, a pair of boots, found on the skeleton, matched those in a rare photograph of the hanging of James Daniels on March 2, 1866.[20]

The city's first formal burial ground opened in March of 1865 on the highest point overlooking the gulch. The death of Dr. L. Rodney Pococke necessitated the cemetery's founding. Pococke was a medical doctor who came west suffering from tuberculosis, hoping the mountain air would cure him. Life in a log cabin under the most primitive conditions in freezing weather, however, spelled his demise. He was reputedly the first person buried in the city cemetery. He was a Mason and like William Bell of

18. Construction of Central School, center, prompted partial removal of Helena's first cemetery. Undisturbed fenced cemetery plots lie behind the school. Bird's-eye map of Helena, 1875. Library of Congress.

Bannack, requested a Masonic funeral. It was largely attended, and citizens named Rodney Street after him. The location of his grave site, however, is unknown. This cemetery served as the main community cemetery until 1875 and likely a portion of it was used after that. Although the site has been developed, its location within the National Register–listed Helena Historic District, remains in the public memory.[21]

Coulson and Elkhorn

The town of Coulson was not a mining camp, but rather a river town on the north bank of the Yellowstone that thrived from 1877 to the mid-1880s. Arrival of the Northern Pacific doomed the town and prompted the founding of Billings nearby. Named

Death in Early Communities

for the Coulson line of steamboats, the short-lived community had a violent history where numerous residents died "with their boots on." Coulson's "Boot Hill" today sits in an unlovely urban setting above Billings's busy Main Street, about a mile east of the present-day downtown. Listed in the National Register, it includes an unknown number of graves. Eventually the burial ground was little more than a pasture. However, it was not forgotten. An obelisk marked the site in 1921 and in the 1970s, Boy Scouts added rows of crosses, not necessarily on the actual graves.[22]

Physicians in nineteenth-century Montana considered the definition of epidemic to be five cases of the same disease. Such ravages knew no social boundaries. The great silver camp of Elkhorn that flourished in the 1880s and early 1890s has a particularly pathetic legacy, recalling that sometimes the sacrifices of parents—leaving home and family for new opportunities—were minor compared to the sacrifices they imposed on their children. Elkhorn's cemetery, perched high above the town on a wooded slope, graphically tells this story.

Dr. William Dudley served as camp doctor but could do nothing when a diphtheria epidemic in 1889 claimed most of Elkhorn's children. Diphtheria was a relentless disease and a terrible way to watch a child die as the characteristic suffocating, grayish membrane crept across the throat. Little could be done to alleviate suffering. Dr. Dudley's wife was pregnant with their second child when the Dudleys left Elkhorn abruptly. They left their firstborn son, a casualty of the epidemic, buried in an unmarked grave on the wooded hillside. He was in company with at least ten other children who died of diphtheria during the spring and summer of 1889.[23]

Later that September, Harry Walton, nine, and Albin Nelson, ten, had somehow escaped the epidemic. They found a quicksilver container full of black powder. Adults filled these containers to detonate for community celebrations and had apparently overlooked this one. As the boys experimented with the powder, they exploded the container and blew themselves to bits. They share a grave in the small cemetery because it was impossible to identify their individual remains.[24]

19. Diphtheria claimed most of Elkhorn's children including the Roberts' two young daughters. Note the grammatical error ("Here lies the sweetest buds . . .") on the epitaph. Photograph by Larry Goldsmith.

Montana's Cemetery Heritage

Hundreds of early cemeteries lie hidden across Montana's vast plains where homesteaders left family plots. Small burial grounds still cling to mountainsides where miners searched for fortune. They, along with their wives or children, oftentimes instead paid the ultimate price. The dead sleep in cemeteries of cities and towns that did not survive. Their fences have fallen, their wooden headboards decayed, and the occasional tombstones have broken. Landowners sometimes sensitively caretake these places and sometimes they do survive by luck. Cemetery Island, representative of the early community of Canyon Ferry in Lewis and Clark County, is one such example.

The mining camp and supply center of Canyon Ferry sprang up at a convenient Missouri River crossing in the 1860s. The community looked to the highest point to establish its burial ground. Old timers recall following the horse-drawn wagon carrying the deceased up the long hill to attend graveside funerals. By the 1940s, rolling grasslands surrounded the cemetery where many of the first local settlers had been buried. Construction of Canyon Ferry Dam in 1953 prompted flooding the area, covering all traces of early settlement. Because of its location on high ground, the cemetery survived and is the only remnant of a once vibrant community. Cemetery Island, surrounded by deep blue waters, is today accessible only by boat. Most, but not all, of the more than eighty burials are marked. Descendants of Canyon Ferry pioneers continue to occasionally bury loved ones there.

The Dearborn Crossing Cemetery in Lewis and Clark County, the Diamond City Cemetery in Broadwater County, and the Blackfoot City Cemetery in Powell County represent the small, inactive early burial grounds that today lie hidden on remote hilltops, tucked in valleys and canyons, or exposed in pastures and prairies but are otherwise preserved in natural decay. They have survived thanks to their inaccessibility and the protection of their owners. These cemeteries recall the difficulties and remoteness of life in the early territory.

The Dearborn Crossing was a stage stop serving travelers and freighters on the road between Fort Benton and Helena. The settlement included a large hotel, livery, general store, and other businesses. Dearborn Crossing was abandoned when the railroad bypassed it in the mid-1880s. The Dearborn Crossing Cemetery sits on a high, flat knoll overlooking the Dearborn River about a mile from the present Highway 287 Bridge. A fence, built by property owners in 1960 to protect the tombstones from cattle, surrounds a portion of the cemetery. Depressions in the ground indicate that there are unmarked graves outside the fence. It is a beautiful, peaceful place that belies the tales of early-day trag-edies its silent residents could tell. Murder, accidents, and sick-ness speak to the hardships of Dearborn pioneers.

In 1866, Charlie Carson was ambushed by Indians one morning as he fetched the stage horses. He was the first person buried in the Dearborn Crossing Cemetery. At least four others subsequently buried there met the same fate. Other tragic stories among the other sixteen known burials between 1866 and 1887 include a fatal lightning strike, measles which led to pneumonia, and blood loss from an accidental ax wound. Most intriguing, however, are the gruesome deaths of William and Hattie Moore in 1885. The deaths were fraught with gossip and inuendo over Mrs. Moore's alleged relationship with a boarder. Although the coroner ruled the deaths murder-suicide, unanswered questions clouded the ruling.[25]

Diamond City, a bustling gold camp founded in 1865, peaked at five thousand people, but by the mid-1880s like so many min-ing camps, its heyday had ended. Similarly, the mining camp of Blackfoot City, contemporary with Diamond City, was the hub of the Ophir Mining District and flourished with a thousand resi-dents. Blackfoot City survived despite numerous fires until 1912. These two cemeteries are typical of mining camps. Several ancient picket fences mark a few individual plots and sparsely scattered headstones identify the two primitive burial grounds. A simple barbed wire fence encircles the Diamond City Cemetery, also known as the Boulder Bar Cemetery. Most of the dozens of buri-als in both these primitive, haphazard graveyards are unmarked.

Some established communities founded less formal burial grounds that continue in use. Libby, the seat of Lincoln County, began as a mining camp that moved to its present location with the advent of the Great Northern Railway in 1892. The Libby Cem-etery has more than six thousand interments. But the town also has a lovely, more informal burial ground. The first interment at Boyd Cemetery, locally known as "Boot Hill," did not occur until 1917 with the death of Adam Boyd. Some eighty-five graves, many of them recent, lie scattered among tall, fragrant pines.

SEVEN

Dead and Buried Twice

Random Graves and Abandoned Cemeteries

A proper burial ground, along with churches and schools, was one of the first signs of a stable and educated community. "Boot hills" were necessarily haphazard and usually not permanent, prompting many western communities to either abandon or relocate their early cemeteries. Anaconda in Deer Lodge County is one example. The original cemetery east of town, used by local ranching families, predated the 1883 founding of Anaconda. In 2005, the abandoned cemetery sat in the middle of the nation's largest Superfund site. Little remained of the undocumented burial ground except an aged juniper tree, an iron cross, tumbled and broken tombstones, and sunken, uneven ground. Some six hundred graves were supposedly relocated in 1910 to make room for expansion of the smelter works.[1]

Relocating a graveyard, even if it is small, is not a pleasant task, but it is much more unsettling to encounter coffins and human remains unexpectedly. Cemeteries and family burials lie forgotten under roads, fields, housing developments, shopping centers, and other urban areas. Nearly every Montana community has abandoned cemeteries and random burials where the dead rest overlooked and undisturbed. Development encroaching upon once-pastoral landscapes can expose the dead. In the mid-1960s, for example, as the Army Corps of Engineers prepared to begin construction of the Libby Dam, twenty-one graves were identified for relocation. Three of them were members of the same family, but the others were single, isolated graves.[2]

Sometimes isolated grave sites along roadways or in public places, like the Thomas family massacre site, are well marked and documented. Sometimes these sites are only known to locals and cared for by groups or individuals who pass the duty on to the next generation. Mystery, for example, shrouds "Charity" Jane Dillon, whose life and death are speculative. But her grave site—marked and remarked several times since 1872—lies carefully tended, tucked along Old Woman's Grave Road between Townsend and Radersburg in Broadwater County. In Meagher County, a neat, white picket fence surrounds the well-tended grave of Alexander Campbell, who died in 1891. A tall wooden obelisk marks his isolated grave at the top of Kings Hill Pass off Route 89 on Forest Service land. Although details of his life may have been lost, his grave has not been forgotten.

Occasionally the dead surface and when they do, they make grisly surprises for those unaware of the history that lies beneath. Forgotten cemeteries sometimes teach us much about the past and sometimes they raise questions that have no answers. A few of these circumstances in various Montana communities illustrate the challenge of forgotten cemeteries and burials and what they may reveal.

Missoula

The Missoula Valley in western Montana was a natural corridor and thus for thousands of years it was a place of Native American travel, especially on the way to hunt buffalo. It was also a place of fierce conflict among local tribes. The eastern end where the land narrowed saw so many ambushes that the area was strewn with human bones. French fur trappers called the area "*Porte d' Enfer*," or "Hell's Gate" until it was renamed "Missoula" in the mid-1860s. While Montana's Native tribes did not usually establish cemeteries or bury their dead, remains have periodically surfaced locally.

During the excavation of the site for the Safeway store on West Broadway in 1950, workers uncovered a small wooden box with the skeleton of a child, predating 1865 by several decades. In 1952, boys digging a cave unearthed the skeleton of a woman

20. Wooden headboards at the base of Mount Jumbo document Missoula's first cemetery. Bird's-eye map of Missoula, 1884. Library of Congress.

buried with ornamental beads, brass jewelry, dyed buckskin clothing and a coiled brass-and-wire ring wrapped around a finger. As late as 2005, "ancient bones" came to light during the excavation for the Rocky Mountain Elk Foundation headquarters on Grant Creek, an area long known for its Native (scaffold) burials and associated artifacts.[3] These testify to Native American travelers through the region before white encroachment.

Beginning circa 1866, the Missoula community's early dead were buried at the base of Mount Jumbo in what is now the National Register–listed Lower Rattlesnake Historic District, between present-day Poplar and Cherry streets. The earlier Hell Gate cemetery, containing some forty burials, as previously discussed, was discontinued and eventually abandoned. Typical of this early time period, there are no burial records, but the Rattlesnake-area cemetery was in regular use by the city until the mid-1880s, when the Missoula City Cemetery opened. A few family members reportedly moved loved ones from the Rattle-snake cemetery to the new city cemetery. The city developed a residential neighborhood on top of the former burial ground as shown in a plat map of 1889. The city approved development over the cemetery in 1891.[4]

Community lore insists that only the Chinese continued to use the old cemetery after 1884. However, as Missoula began to keep better burial records, two non-Chinese interments in the old cemetery were recorded in the 1890s. Newspapers also report several elaborate Chinese funerals with burials in the Rattlesnake cemetery during the decade.[5] Chinese custom dictated that bodies be temporarily interred and after some time, the bones were disinterred and returned to China. Evidence of this practice surfaced in 1937 as WPA crews leveled Cherry Street. A silver handle about five feet down came to light. Further investigation revealed a casket with a pair of trousers, a silk kimono, and shoes along with a burial brick inscribed in Chinese, translated as "Lee Foo Lim is buried here." The casket, however, contained no bones, indicating that the remains were likely returned to China.[6]

Most current homeowners along Cherry Street are aware that there could be human remains buried beneath their properties. In 1974, one Cherry Street resident was excavating his backyard in preparation for an addition onto his house when the backhoe turned up a human skeleton. The coroner initially assumed this was another Chinese burial. However, that did not prove to be the case. The county coroner determined that there were two sets of bones encased in the decayed wood of two old-fashioned coffins. The remains, along with pieces of metal hardware and splintered wood, were turned over to the University of Montana's Anthropology Department where several generations of anthropology students studied them.[7] Over the years, students solved some of the mystery, determining that one individual was a child and the other a female adult. Hardware fragments were consistent with nineteenth-century coffin styles. But whose eternal sleep was so rudely interrupted?

Combining historical records with forensics, one student proposed a theory. The style of the coffin (narrow at the feet, widen-

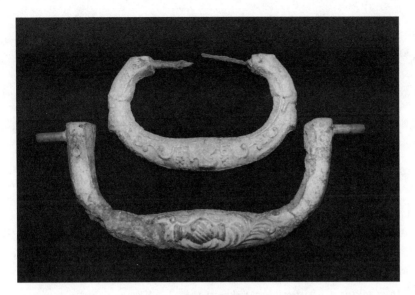

21. Coffin hardware from the old Missoula cemetery helped date remains.
Photograph by Katie Baumler.

ing at the shoulders) and its silver handles were consistent with
the 1870s–1880s. Analysis of the adult bones revealed the person to
be between twenty-five and thirty-four years old. The person had
a poor diet and porosity of the bones that could indicate tuberculosis. General Land Office (GLO) records document the landowners during the 1870s and 1880s. Combining this information
with early newspapers yielded a possible identity of the female
adult. In 1871–72, Cyrus McWhirk owned the land on which the
cemetery was located. On May 9, 1872, Henrietta McWhirk Harrison, who was visiting her brothers Cyrus and William McWhirk,
died of "consumption," the common term for tuberculosis. Mrs.
Harrison had been in delicate health for some time before she
departed Ohio for Montana. She contracted a cold after a perilous journey by stage from Corinne, Utah, to Missoula.[8] Scientific
analysis of the bones, including testing for tuberculosis, could further strengthen the hypothesis that the skeleton was that of Henrietta Harrison. As teaching tools at the university, the bones of the
two unidentified individuals have served an important function
allowing physical anthropology students hands-on experience.

The prominent ridge where Helena's first cemetery located has been disturbed multiple times and burials have surfaced there. The demise of Dr. L. Rodney Pococke, mentioned previously, precipitated the cemetery's founding on the town's most visible vantage point. Among other early interments were Argyle Parkinson, infant son of William and Jeannette Parkinson in May 1865 and ten-year-old Anna Davenport in September 1865. Argyle died of "brain fever" (probably encephalitis or meningitis) and Anna died of a lingering case of measles contracted aboard the steamship St. John as the family traveled from Missouri to Fort Benton.[9]

In 1875, as Helena became Montana's territorial capital, officials determined that the cemetery's strategic location was the best place to build Central School, the first graded school in Montana Territory. Marked graves, including those of Argyle Parkinson and Anna Davenport, and many others encountered in digging the school's foundation, were moved to the county cemetery on Benton Avenue. But many graves were not moved, and the old city cemetery continued in minimal use.

In 1893, as the first Helena High School was under construction at Lawrence and Warren streets next to Central School, children sat on the hill during recess and watched as workmen discovered many nameless bodies.[10] As late as 1983, road crews discovered human remains northwest of the schoolyard during the construction of Cruse Avenue. Like the 1974 discovery on Cherry Street in Missoula, the immediate reaction was that the burial was Chinese. A University of Montana anthropologist, however, concluded that the skeleton was Caucasian. The body was encased in the remains of a sturdy hardwood coffin and the nails dated to around the turn of the twentieth century, proving that the cemetery was in use for some time after 1875, and not necessarily by the Chinese as many assumed.[11]

The old city cemetery and "boot hill," where several burials have surfaced, are not the only urban places in Helena where remains have come to light and created problems. St. Mary's

Catholic Cemetery on Oakes Street was in use from the 1860s until it was abandoned in the early 1900s. In the 1970s, the city acquired the dilapidated property and created Robinson Park. Families had the opportunity to relocate loved ones, but at least 1,065 graves remained undisturbed. Broken pieces of tombstones were bulldozed and gathered to be dumped. Intact headstones were set up at the current Resurrection Cemetery and can be found today along the east perimeter in the Lazarus West section. No bodies are associated with these stones.

Remains have surfaced several times outside Robinson Park when crews installing water and gas mains removed street paving. In 2004, several caskets came to light including one child's casket with a viewing window and the words "Our Darling" embossed upon it. Likewise, more excavating uncovered some seven caskets on Livingston Avenue bordering the park in 2018.[12]

Clancy

Public memory is sometimes much like a game of "gossip" that begins with a whispered phrase and by the time it reaches the last person, it hardly resembles the original. Perceptions handed down sometimes become convincing community "truths" that are difficult to dispel. One such example is the apocryphal story about an ancient Ponderosa pine at Clancy in Jefferson County where some claim vigilantes hung "dozens" of miscreants. It is a gruesome fact that even during the earliest period of Montana's settlement, journals, newspapers, and even photographs documented hangings. Not a shred of evidence exists that the tree was used for such purpose, and further, Jefferson County saw only six hangings. Five were legal and one was conducted by the miner's court. Four occurred at the county courthouse in Boulder between 1889 and 1925 and two at Radersburg in 1871 and 1878.[13] A fence around the base of the tree has been mistakenly interpreted and does not define a cemetery as tourists and others commonly assume. There are no graves there. However, in June 2005, a shocking mystery did present itself to the small Clancy community.

The excavation of a basement for one of the first homes built in Clancy's newly-platted Red Cliff Estates yielded a grisly discov-

22. A backhoe digging a basement for a home in Clancy's Red Cliff Estates
subdivision hit a metal casket, dislodging human remains.
Photograph by Sheriff Craig Doolittle.

ery when the backhoe operator hit a metal casket. The impact
broke the glass viewing window—a common feature in nineteenth-
century caskets. The backhoe operator promptly quit when the
skull rolled out of its longtime resting place. Speculation was that
this was a female since her long dark hair had been twisted into
a bun, but there was no other hint at the person's identity. Jefferson County Sheriff Craig Doolittle arrived on the scene and
carefully photographed the casket—which also featured expensive silver handles—and the human remains. The sheriff sent
the photos to the Department of Anthropology at the University of Montana.

Anxious to discover more about the remains, Sheriff Doolittle
contacted Charleen Spalding, whose skills as a graveyard detective
are locally well-known. Her intensive research potentially identified the deceased. Family of the longtime owners of Red Cliff
Farm, which spanned the 1890s into the twentieth century, knew
of no burials in what had been a farmers' field before the subdivision. But the history was older than the 1890s. The historic
farmhouse, built by its original owners, Silas S. and Frances Har-

vey, still stood at the edge of the property. The Harveys founded Red Cliff Farm and built the house in the early 1870s. The Harveys bred and raised expensive trotting horses they brought to Montana from Kentucky. The Helena newspapers yielded information about the Harveys and several family deaths that occurred during their ownership. The Harveys' three-year-old granddaughter, Esta Clara Eddy, died of diphtheria in 1883. Mortuary records revealed her burial at Benton Avenue Cemetery. Frances Harvey's mother, Rebecca Addis, died in 1888 and was buried next to Esta Clara. Other family deaths included Silas Harvey in 1879 and the Harveys' daughter, Evelyn Mae Harvey Eddy, in 1887. There is no record of either of these burials.

University of Montana anthropologists confirmed that the skull was that of a female. Putting all the evidence together, it seemed likely that the body was that of Evelyn Eddy. The body and casket were quietly reburied in the Clancy cemetery and the case closed.[14] The location of Silas Harvey's burial has not been discovered, but it would be logical for him to be buried somewhere near his daughter. The case illustrates the common practice of burial on private property and that human remains can surface in unexpected places.

Dillon

The cemetery history of Dillon in Beaverhead County follows the familiar urban pattern. The town, founded in 1880, was the terminus of the Union Pacific Railroad. Its first cemetery was relocated to the more formal Mountain View Cemetery in the late 1880s. Nearly two decades passed. In October 1907, road graders working just inside the Dillon city limits unearthed thirteen bodies that had been buried in the city's first cemetery. These thirteen either originally lay in unmarked graves or had markers that had long deteriorated. Workers gathered the scattered bones, placing two individuals to a coffin, and reburied them in Mountain View. The discovery prompted arguments between the city and the county. The graves were unearthed a few feet outside the city limits by city workers. The city claimed that since the remains were found in the county, the county should pay for the removal and reburials. The county attorney, however, said otherwise: "If the city goes outside its limits and digs up something that does not belong to it, it is the city's funeral." Curiously, workers also discovered the remains of two large dogs and a hog. Each had been carefully placed in its own pine box and buried.[15] Only one human identity among the group could be determined.

One coffin yielded part of a skull that had been wrapped in cloth and paper and placed at the foot of the deceased. Strands of long dark hair and items of clothing revealed the person's identity and recalled a horrific tragedy. In August 1883, Evangeline "Eva Clark" Bird, a talented fifteen-year-old musician and actress, was working as an assistant to Charles Lewis, a well-known magician and sleight-of-hand expert. She had been traveling with him, with her mother's permission, as he performed around the region. The pair was preparing to move on when Eva went to the wagon to get a cap from a trunk to complete her traveling outfit. As she moved items aside, a loaded gun accidentally discharged and blew off half her head. Officials first thought that Professor Lewis had pulled the trigger. The scene was ghastly and Lewis incoherent. He was promptly arrested and charged with first degree premeditated murder. However, several people vouched for Lewis's fine character, and Eva's mother wrote a letter stating that Lewis was like a father to her daughter and had always done right by her. W. Y. Pemberton, who later served as Chief Justice of the Montana Supreme Court (1893–99), was one of the defense attorneys. Lewis was found not guilty.[16] Evangeline Bird was reburied in Mountain View Cemetery and her grave marked.

Another removal to Mountain View involves the personal life of Montana's famous itinerant Methodist minister, William Wesley Van Orsdel, known to most as "Brother Van." His travels in the 1870s included the Beaverhead Valley where he visited the sheep ranch of Richard Reynolds. Reynolds's wife, Virginia, was the sister of Phillip Poindexter of the famous Poindexter-Orr Ranch. Virginia's first husband had died leaving her with three children to raise and Reynolds loved them as his own. The Reynoldses soon became a fixture on Brother Van's route. Virginia's daughter, thirteen-year-year-old Jennie Johnston, and Brother Van became fast friends. When Jennie turned eighteen, Brother Van was thirty-one. They were engaged, but Virginia wanted Jennie to attend college. So in September 1879, they put their wedding plans on hold and Jennie boarded the stage for Northwest University in Evanston, Illinois. Jennie's college plans, however, dissolved when she became ill with tuberculosis. Her health was up and down until the summer of 1881 when her condition worsened, and the end came in October. Brother Van was heartbroken. Jennie lay in her coffin in the Reynolds's parlor. As Brother Van sat with her keeping vigil, he quietly took the ring he would have given her at their marriage and slipped it on her finger. He never married, and always wore the wedding ring Jennie would have given him.[17]

Jennie was originally buried in the Poindexter family cemetery, which predated Dillon and served the local ranching community. Forty-three graves remain in the Poindexter Cemetery, which today lies unceremoniously in a farmer's field. Jennie's grave was moved to Dillon's Mountain View Cemetery and her tombstone has been lost; a small metal nameplate marks her final resting place. Brother Van accomplished great good and visited his Jennie's grave every year of his long life including the year he died in 1919. He is buried in Forestvale Cemetery at Helena.

Big Timber to Zortman

Oliver Peter Zortman was among the few hopeful miners to extract a small fortune in gold from the Little Rocky Mountains in Eastern Montana. He came west in 1888 and struck it rich, founding the Alabama Mine. His name would have been lost except that it lives on in the town he founded. His fortune, however, dwindled and his wife and daughters dispersed to California. Zortman found some solace in Masonry, joining the fraternal organization in Chinook. His wife, Rose and two grown daughters, Helen and Lulu, rejoined him for a time in Big Timber in the early 1930s but by 1933, his family had returned to California and he was ill with cancer. Like most gold miners who were a product of the western rushes, Zortman ended his days penniless. He died in the hospital at Big Timber, a ward of the county.[18] In addition to his wife and daughters, Zortman left a brother in Pennsylvania, but no family attended his funeral. Photographs, however, of the open casket were taken on their behalf. He was buried in the pauper's section in a hand-dug, unmarked grave.

A few years ago, residents determined to honor their namesake by bringing his remains back to Zortman. The unmarked grave in Big Timber's Mountain View Cemetery was not easy to locate. His membership in the Masons at Chinook offered clues that led to a leather-bound ledger at the Big Timber Masonic Lodge. The book gave a few details of Zortman's funeral and the possible location of his grave. With permission from Zortman's relatives, several veterinarians, a Chinook undertaker, cemetery workers, and assorted Zortman residents oversaw the exhumation. The remains of Pete Zortman were not easy to extract. The chocolate-colored soil was damp from a nearby irrigation ditch, and as soon as the backhoe bit into the soil, the hole flooded. After removing three feet of muck, artifacts including a Masonic apron surfaced. Soon pieces of the casket, and then bones, began to emerge. Most of Zortman's yellowed bones were collected and placed in a sturdy pine box and loaded into a truck destined for Pete's namesake.

A weekend of festivities surrounded Pete Zortman's second funeral on August 27, 2005. A vintage hearse carried the pine box from the tiny town to its local cemetery, but unlike the last time, a smattering of relatives, along with most of Zortman's sixty-some residents, attended the graveside services. A distant relative later wrote to the *Billings Gazette* about Pete Zortman's relocation, noting that she had visited his unmarked grave in Big Timber and found the cemetery a most beautiful spot. But she also noted that the exit sign off I-90 for Mountain View Cemetery read Dead End. She added that fortunately it was not quite the end of the road for Pete.[19]

EIGHT

The Evolution of Beautiful Burial Grounds

Paris Sets the Trend

Places where people live permanently have always included places to bury the dead. But large, planned, and landscaped cemeteries were not on the minds of western pioneers. Cemeteries of beauty evolved only as settlements became more permanent and the population less transient. They were a product of necessity, but also of a population with more leisure time, the need to recreate, and the need for artistic expression. Drawing upon the "garden park" movement, Montana's larger cities began to cultivate parklike cemeteries with formal landscaping and sculptured monuments. The idea, however, did not spring from American creativity; rather the first formal, parklike cemeteries were of European invention.

In large European urban areas, churchyard and private family burials over many generations eventually became grossly over-full. This, along with other circumstances, reached a crisis in eighteenth-century Paris. The practice was to deny Christian burial to executed criminals. The unfortunate victims, of which there were many, were usually hung and left to rot where they died. Further, when epidemics caused so many deaths that the corpses could not be properly buried, bodies were dumped in the sewers. These practices created extreme health hazards. The terrible stench of human decay was unbearable and the potential for spreading disease extreme. Residents feared the *miasmas*, or clouds, of stinking air that permeated Parisian streets and alleyways.

The city finally acted. Under cover of night during the winters between 1785 and 1787, the remains of thousands buried in small cemeteries throughout Paris were removed to the underground catacombs, a labyrinth beneath the city where thieves and cut-throats kept their hideouts. Cemeteries on the outskirts of Paris replaced these inner-city burial grounds. One of the first was the famous Père Lachaise Cemetery, which opened in 1804. Drawing upon beautiful landscaped English gardens, the innovative planners of Père Lachaise applied these principles to a cemetery for the first time. Its natural rural setting, planned walkways, and funerary art attracted international attention.[1]

Père Lachaise was different from all other cemeteries in another important way. The common practice for the middle class was to rent burial space for six to twenty years. After this time, the remains were disinterred and removed to the charnel house, a receptacle for storing bones to make room for other burials. The concept of perpetual care was unheard of until Père Lachaise allowed middle class families to purchase perpetual burial rights. This cemetery fostered a greater respect for the dead.[2]

Cemeteries in the United States

Burial trends in the United States followed European models for like reasons. There were no large cemeteries before the 1830s, but the same problems arose: small urban burial places and church-yard grounds became over-crowded. Walls collapsed during flooding, sometimes sending generations of burials, one on top of another, out into the open. Horrific scenes of floating coffins and exposed remains—a mixture dubbed "bone gumbo" in the South—reminiscent of the horrors of Paris were equally disgusting to their American counterparts. During times of smallpox, cholera, typhoid, and yellow fever epidemics, exposed remains brought well-founded fears of spreading diseases. Cities became more crowded, real estate costs rose, and "cemeteries were seen as the last great necessity."[3]

Beginning in the 1830s, Americans began to view cemeteries in a new light. In 1831, construction of Mount Auburn Cemetery at Cambridge, Massachusetts, began a movement to establish expansive, planned cemeteries. Rural, landscaped cemeteries alleviated crowded, unhealthy urban burial grounds and provided a place for families to enjoy a parklike setting while commemorating their loved ones. Residents flocked to the new "garden park," and Mount Auburn became the model for other cities. Philadelphia's Laurel Hill in 1836; Green Mount Cemetery in Baltimore, Maryland, in 1838; and Green-Wood Cemetery overlooking Manhattan in Brooklyn, New York, in 1839 were the first among many others that followed suit during the mid-nineteenth century. These new cemeteries provided a solution to the age-old problem of what to do with the dead, setting a trend to return to the ideas of the Greeks and Romans, who buried their loved ones out of town, away from urban areas.

Rural garden cemeteries provided America's first public open spaces where all were welcome and inspired the American Park movement. They became galleries where visitors could soak up culture. Chapels, monuments, and mausoleums on the grounds offered wonderful opportunities for the display of art in the form of architecture, sculpture, and stained glass. The family mausoleum was an expression of wealth and social status. Made popular by Queen Victoria after the death of her husband Albert in 1861, these tombs gained in popularity in cemeteries across the United States. Garden park cemeteries were educational. Young people could learn from the accomplishments of ancestors and others and find direction for their own lives. Death was a familiar companion in the nineteenth century, and most children were exposed to death at an early age. Mothers could take their children to the cemetery to "instill a cheerful association with death," negating the usual connotations, so children would not be afraid.[4]

Rural garden cemeteries evolved into the "lawn" and "memorial park" cemetery movement from about 1855 to 1920. The lawn cemetery in the later nineteenth century included driveways instead of walking paths and great expanses of open grassy areas. Lawn cemeteries employed flush markers that left the lawn visually intact or other types of regulated markers. In the twentieth century, lawn cemeteries became memorial cemeteries with the addition of perpetual care under a nonprofit or business organization.[5]

The desire for beautiful cemeteries was well underway nationally as the 1870s closed. By that time in Montana Territory, the initial frenzy of the gold rush had ended, and the population was becoming much less transient. Community stability meant that residents remained longer in one place and were therefore better able to care for the final resting places of loved ones. With a new sense of civic responsibility in growing towns and cities came a desire for attractive communities and the need to mark grave sites. Montana already had many abandoned burial grounds and hundreds of unmarked graves. It was a fertile ground for stonecutters and there was money to be made in manufacturing monuments and tombstones.

Before Montana had its own manufacturers, and even after, marble and granite tombstones and the companion footstones—with the deceased's initials delineating the end of the grave—came from major suppliers like Sullivan and Farnham's Marble and Granite Monuments in Minneapolis and from as far away as New York. Until marble could be imported and local granite quarries developed, mail-order markers or locally carved wooden headboards were the options for those who wished to formally mark a grave. Imported white marble mail-order upright tombstones and obelisk monuments from the 1870s and 1880s and occasional wooden headboards dot Montana's early historic cemeteries. These evocative memorials chronicle the earliest decades of territorial history.

The other early tombstone option was zinc. Many Montana cemeteries include beautiful examples of these hollow metal markers. Commonly called "white bronze," the Monumental Bronze Company in Bridgeport, Connecticut, was the first to produce these versatile markers and eventually had subsidiaries in numerous states. Monumental Bronze made monuments as well as tombstones. Available from 1874 to 1914, white bronze was very lightweight, durable, easy to ship and assemble, less expensive, and could be highly personalized. The characteristic blue-gray stone-like finish was achieved through a process of sandblasting the cast pieces and then brushing them with a chemical. In 1892, E. S. Hall of Billings was the Montana and Idaho agent. The company advertised that the durability of the product was scientifically endorsed.[6] Zinc tombstones were unique to the Victorian era and were popular for about forty years.

Larger, extant pioneer cemeteries like Virginia City's Hillside, the Demersville and St. Mary's Mission cemeteries, the tiny Mac-Donald family cemetery at Fort Connah, and Helena's Benton Avenue, feature a simple square or rectangular layout. If the cemetery was large enough, a central wagon road or pathway separated the two halves of the grounds. Larger pioneer cemeteries like Benton Avenue often have a secondary road or pathway dividing the cemetery into four quadrants. Families were responsible for planting and caring for their own plots and therefore they are often delineated with wood or wrought iron fencing, some type of curbing, and historic plantings such as lilacs or evergreens.

As Montana Territory began to establish permanent communities, by the early 1880s, tombstone makers were at work producing headstones and monuments. The arrival of the Northern Pacific Railway in 1883 made shipping heavy items much more feasible. Before that, bull teams pulling thousand-pound freight wagons transported suitable materials. Montana's first marble works may have been Kirkaldie and Carr, who advertised in December of 1878 that their shop in Helena had a stock of American and Italian marble and that they would be promptly filling orders for tombstones across the territory. In 1880, Thomas and Sandberg produced a handsome monument to advertise their stonecutting business in Butte and in 1881, Daniel Dutro and J. F. Kielhauer founded the Benton Stone and Marble Works in Fort Benton.[7] George Pringle came from Minneapolis to found the Missoula Marble Works in the later 1880s. Stone artist O. F. Smith, along with F. X. Gasselin and Edgar Morgan, came from Chicago around 1889 to form the Montana Marble Works in Helena. Alonzo K. Prescott's marble works at Helena and Butte, however, supplied most Montana tombstones of imported marble or locally quar-

23. A. K. Prescott's business signature, like this one in Virginia City's Hillside Cemetery, appears on tombstones throughout Montana. Photograph by Larry Goldsmith.

ried granite from the mid-1880s into the early twentieth century. An advertisement in 1887 claimed that there probably was not a churchyard in Montana that did not display Prescott's work.[8] By the end of the 1880s, Prescott's business had produced more than three thousand tombstones.

Alonzo K. Prescott was born December 18, 1851, in New Hampshire. He left home at fifteen to find work and in 1874 traveled west to Colorado. He started a store and served several terms as postmaster from 1879 to 1882 at the boomtown of Rico, Colorado. In 1882, he answered an ad in the *Denver Post* placed by a couple in Helena looking to start a stonecutting business. Prescott arrived in August of 1883, just before the east and west halves of the Northern Pacific met at Independence, near Gold Creek, Montana. According to family recollections, he had to hire a man to carry his luggage a mile across the gap. Once in Helena, he discovered that the husband of the couple had died, but Prescott was already committed to the business. Prescott's son recounted how his father figured he had better learn something about the business, so he went back to Boston for six months to educate himself in the art of stone cutting. Returning to Montana via the Northern Pacific with a load of marble, he hired an expert stone-cutter on his way through Minneapolis. Prescott bought property near Helena's Northern Pacific yards in February 1884 and had opened his marble works by June. He got his start in the business traveling the countryside on horseback and by buggy, taking tombstone orders.[9] Soon he opened a branch in Butte, later operated by his nephew, Leland Prescott. The Prescotts dominated the business until about 1905.

Other firms opened in cities across Montana. By 1890, F. X. Gasselin of the Montana Marble Works in Helena was taking many tombstone orders in Billings.[10] The firm competed with Prescott, but these firms and others in Helena and Butte established the two towns as Montana's tombstone headquarters. While individual tombstone artists did not usually sign their work, Prescott's company signature appears on many Montana tombstones from Bozeman to Corvallis and into Northern Idaho. Prescott himself, however, was not the artist and probably never did any stone carving. Similar company signatures for the Montana Marble Works and the Missoula Marble Works and others appear on tombstones and monuments made by those firms.

Montana Catches Up

Montana's early cemeteries, like those across the newly settled West, suffered the same overcrowding, urban encroachment, and decay as their eastern counterparts. Montana's cities and towns grew rapidly, especially after 1883, when the Northern Pacific Railway made settlement in the territory less difficult. Montana began to catch up to the national trends. Sealed metal caskets became more popular, required for shipping remains long distances by rail.

Cemetery parks developed in the later nineteenth and early twentieth centuries. As at Mount Auburn, they were public places where residents went to enjoy the beauty of nature, recreate, and reflect. Bozeman's Sunset Hills, Billings's Mountview, and Butte's Mount Moriah evolved from smaller cemeteries into larger, beautifully landscaped, tended parks. Missoula's City Cemetery in 1885, Helena's Forestvale Cemetery in 1890, and Kalispell's C. E. Conrad Memorial Cemetery in 1903, were architecturally planned and landscaped and serve as Montana's prototypes.

Sunset Hills Cemetery, now maintained under Bozeman Parks and Recreation, was established at Bozeman in 1872 on a scant five acres of treeless land. Wealthy English philanthropist Lord William Blackmore and his wife, Mary, had just arrived at Bozeman, traveling from Colorado. They intended to accompany geologist Ferdinand V. Hayden on an expedition Blackmore had helped finance into newly created Yellowstone National Park. Fatigue from travel and sudden weather change brought on a "congestive chill" and Mary died suddenly of pneumonia on July 18, 1872.[11] Lord Blackmore purchased land on which to bury his wife and donated it to the city. Mary Blackmore was thus the first buried in what would become Sunset Hills.

Located on East Main Street adjacent to Lindley Park, Sunset Hills was not originally intended as a public parklike cemetery, but rather was informally laid out in typical pioneer fashion. Local women spent hours planting pine trees transplanted from the mountains on the barren hill. Legend has it that they placed small sacks of potatoes in each hole to provide needed moisture. But by the early 1900s, the burial ground became untended and overgrown. In 1910, Elizabeth Bogert helped establish a local cemetery board. Her brother John, five times mayor of Bozeman, had died and was buried there in 1895. Elizabeth saw that water lines were brought in and weeping birch and spruce trees planted, and overgrown graves cleaned and weeded. The parklike ambience, laid out in two gentle rectangles with curved corners, evolved over the early decades of the twentieth century. Today, the park totals seventy-one acres; thirty-eight are in use and include nearly eighteen thousand interments. The lovely rise overlooking Bozeman is not so formal, but a peaceful place of "sunshine and singing birds and old friendships taken up again."[12]

Billings's Mountview Cemetery is the largest and oldest cemetery in the Yellowstone region but did not achieve its present parklike appearance until 1920. The small, private Billings Cemetery adjacent opened circa 1881. The stones of this older section are visually different from those at the newer Mountview. The older portion is laid out in a series of six interlinked circular drives with an original, wide wagon road running north and south. The prominent O'Donnell family founded and maintained this first burial ground. In the 1920s, the city of Billings purchased the Billings Cemetery and neighboring land totaling sixty-five acres and opened Mountview Cemetery. It was then laid out with loop drives winding around sixteen sections. Characteristic of the park cemetery, both natural and planted deciduous and evergreen trees lie along the curving driveways and in natural random fashion enhancing the grounds. The cemetery, at Central Avenue and Regal Street, is adjacent to a golf course on the west side.[13]

While cemeteries were usually located in rural areas partly for aesthetic reasons, in Butte health and sanitation were of extreme concern and location was of the utmost importance. Mining everywhere created ground disturbance and early urban burials did not always remain underground. Two fraternal groups, the Masons and the Oddfellows, founded Mount Moriah on South Montana Street and platted the flat ground in square blocks in 1877. This was Montana's first formally planned cemetery. It initially only included four sections. The block pattern in Butte was less an aesthetic function of the lawn-park movement but more a necessity since there was no landscape to accommodate curving driveways, just flat, barren soil. As much as the community wanted a cemetery that served as a location of beauty, in nineteenth-century Butte this was impossible. Open hearth smelting polluted the area and prevented anything from growing.

The cemetery was bleak and ugly, and individual plot owners cared for their own plots. Butte's citizens, however, made up for the lack of landscaping by placing fanciful and lovely tombstones on their loved ones' graves. Consequently, Butte has the most unique and attractive cemetery art of any Montana city. Although the desire to create "a spot of beauty" was at first far-fetched, by 1905, as smelting centralized in Anaconda, trees and shrubs began to revegetate. The cemetery reincorporated by 1917, installed a water system, and planted four thousand Canadian poplars. The superintendent researched which plants would grow in Butte's soil resulting in the cultivation of seventeen kinds of trees and thirty kinds of shrubs.[14]

The Missoula City Cemetery, with over twenty-one thousand interments, encompasses eighty acres. Half of the grounds are in use and forty acres are reserved for future burials. The cemetery began as a small private burial ground established three miles from the town's center by a group of businessmen in 1881. They purchased the initial fourteen acres from the Northern Pacific Railway for $168. County surveyor Harry V. Wheeler formally platted the cemetery in 1885 in block sections with roads to the outside. One diagonal road bisected the grounds. Alleyways accommodated horses and carriages, and some stations featured large hitching areas in square and circular patterns. The alleyways also accommodated the early irrigation system, which tapped into the fairgrounds once located nearby. The roads bore the names of the virtues (Faith, Hope, and Charity), trees, and flowers. In 1901, the City of Missoula purchased the cemetery for one dollar and appointed a board of six trustees. Its mission was to "develop a tranquil and dignified park setting for the burial of the deceased." The original roads and alleys were somewhat reconfigured in 1925 to accommodate automobile traffic with large, circular roundabouts added to facilitate traffic flow. The board's mission, however, remains the same today.[15]

Lack of space in Helena's National Register–listed Benton Avenue Cemetery and a need to provide beautiful burial grounds for the prominent, wealthy families in Montana's capital prompted city fathers to purchase 160 acres two and a half miles north of Helena. National Register–listed Forestvale Cemetery was a planned parklike cemetery formally designed by civil engineer Harry V. Wheeler in 1890, who previously planned the Missoula City Cemetery. Although the area was bleak and treeless, Wheeler created a natural-looking attractive setting with looping driveways and orderly plot rows following the contours of the graceful loops. He created a small lake with a tiny island and a grand entry gate. The Helena Cemetery Association incorporated, and stockholders included many prominent Helena residents. The Association developed the site, provided landscaping, a water system, and sold plots.[16]

Among these high style Montana cemeteries, the National Register–listed C. E. Conrad Memorial Cemetery deserves foremost discussion. Unlike any other Montana cemetery, it was thoughtfully sited, carefully planned by a professional landscape architect with years of experience in the field of cemetery management and horticulture, and legally organized as a perpetual care facility. While other Montana cemeteries may today appear similar, except for the Missoula and Forestvale cemeteries that were planned, the others evolved into garden parks. The other exceptional feature about the C. E. Conrad Memorial Cemetery is its legal inclusion of perpetual care. Other cemeteries followed suit, but laws passed to allow this feature for the Conrad Cemetery make it unique.

Development of the Conrad Cemetery

Kalispell founder Charles Conrad and his wife Alicia (nicknamed "Lettie"), saw Kalispell grow, and both had great faith in its future. The Conrads agreed that the town's last great necessity was a cemetery, one that would be grand and beautiful and affordable, and most important, open to all residents, regardless of religion, social status, or ethnic origin. During the 1890s, as Kalispell continued to use the old cemetery at Demersville, it became more obvious that the town needed its own burial ground. And Charles Conrad, keenly aware that he was losing his ten-year battle with diabetes, knew that he was running out of time.

One fine sunny autumn afternoon in 1902, he and Lettie rode their horses out to a beautiful promontory overlooking the Whitefish and Stillwater Rivers. It was a favorite haunt they had visited many times and always found it breathtaking. They dismounted and let the horses graze. Charles had never expressed his burial wishes, but at that moment he told his wife he wanted to be buried on this promontory, believing that there could be no more peaceful, lovely spot for final rest.

Charles died several weeks later, but shortly before his death, he directed his attorney to purchase the beautiful point and the ten acres surrounding it. Charles sketched the family mausoleum as he wished it built and positioned it on the grassy outcrop where the land fell steeply to the Stillwater River. Charles's body lay in a temporary receiving vault on the point while the mausoleum underwent construction. His was the cemetery's first interment, but other burials occurred very soon after.[17]

Lettie Conrad purchased the entire eighty-seven-acre promontory. Her vision was for the land to serve as a resting place for all the people of Kalispell and provide perpetual care with a permanent maintenance fund. However, Montana had no legislation allowing for a memorial cemetery with perpetual care.

As Lettie's attorney set to work on legislation, she and her youngest daughter Alicia visited cemeteries across the United States and in Canada and Mexico in search of the right design. Perhaps through the family's association with Great Northern Railway mogul James J. Hill, the Conrads met Arthur W. Hobert, superintendent of Lakewood Cemetery of Minneapolis. Lakewood, founded in 1871, followed the "rural garden" plan and was a nonprofit, nondenominational cemetery as Lettie envisioned. Hobert, a landscape architect, visited Kalispell and commented, "I cannot improve upon God's architecture. My advice is to disturb as little as possible. Do not move a shovelful of earth that is not necessary. You already have one of the most beautiful cemetery sites in the world."[18]

At the very northern tip of the promontory where the family mausoleum was under construction between 1902 and 1908, Lettie had a series of steep stone steps cut into the cliff. The steps, some of which appear to be carved from the outcrop and some hand-laid, switch back at certain points. They lead down from the promontory to a historic carriage road along the Stillwater River. This portion of the hillside is buttressed with concrete and stone retaining walls of the same vintage to prevent undercutting and erosion. Midway down the steps, a stone bench offers rest to the winded climber. The "Fairy Steps" gave Lettie Conrad private access to the family mausoleum. Hugging the base of the promontory, just outside the cemetery boundary line, remnants of the carriage road wind along the valley floor.

24. The legendary Fairy Steps in Kalispell's C. E. Conrad Memorial
Cemetery provided Mrs. Conrad private access to mourn her husband.
Photograph by author.

Charles was never far from Lettie's thoughts. In the evenings
when the day's work was finished, and the weather was good, her
driver harnessed the horses and brought the carriage around.
Lettie would be waiting. They drove the short distance to the
cemetery along the carriage path. Lettie would alight from the
carriage below the narrow point of land and climb the Fairy
Steps to the mausoleum. There she would spend a few min-
utes in quiet meditation at her husband's grave and return to
the carriage seemingly refreshed and reinvigorated. The steps
first served only Lettie and the immediate Conrad family. But as
the carriage road became obsolete with the advent of the auto-
mobile into the 1920s, the steps took on a different purpose.
Generations of Kalispell children visiting the cemetery amused
themselves scampering up and down the "Fairy Steps." The steps
are fraught with myth and legend. Supposedly if you count the
steps going down, and count them again on the way up, the number is never the same.[19]

Today, the cemetery owns enough property to accommodate interments of Kalispell families of all socio-economic levels for the next two hundred years. Located near the eastern edge of the town of Kalispell, it encompasses eighty-seven acres, serves the public, and includes more than 17,850 burials. In addition, planning and legislation that Lettie Conrad insisted upon ensure that the cemetery will never become a "weed patch."[20]

The Conrad Cemetery follows the evolution of the rural garden park concept, integrating three phases characteristic of American rural cemetery evolution. The first phase includes blending the natural environment and vegetation with careful, appropriate horticulture. Winding, hilly pathways follow the contour of the landscape melding both in harmony while artistic tombstones placed in an orderly fashion enhance the grounds. The second phase promotes the cemetery as a parklike lawn retreat where the public can stroll and enjoy the natural surroundings. The third "memorial park" phase required the use of flat, embedded tombstones, which preserves expansive, lawn-like grassy areas, making the lawn seem continuous and pristine. The Conrad Cemetery and its various sections incorporate all three of these design phases. Careful stewardship has ensured that the Conrad Cemetery remains untouched by modern encroachments.[21]

The Conrad Memorial Cemetery paved the way for other Montana cemeteries to offer perpetual care. This feature did not emerge successfully in Montana until after the Conrad model was established and its attendant legislation passed in 1905. Even so, not all cemeteries offer perpetual care, which usually includes general maintenance of the grounds, pathways, and driveways. Forestvale was planned as a perpetual care facility, but because no governing legislation existed in the 1890s, that feature eventually went defunct. While Forestvale does today offer perpetual care options, and it is a garden park cemetery, it is not a memorial lawn cemetery. It has no great sweeps of grassy spaces with embedded markers. The Conrad Cemetery remains Montana's only true garden park/memorial lawn facility.

NINE

Cemetery Diversity

The Eclectic Mix

Montana has hundreds of cemeteries that mirror the state's surprising cultural and social diversity. Chinese, Japanese, African Americans, Germans, Russians, Italians, Irish, English, and myriad others brought their languages and cultures to the remote Montana frontier. They came to work claims, or to "mine the miners" with goods and services, or homestead or ranch or work on the railroad. Religious groups included Catholics, Jews, and Protestants. Within a few years, Montana Territory became one of the most culturally diverse places in the American West. Cemeteries prove that this is so, but burial grounds not only reflect ethnicity and religion, they also document fraternal and social organizations, military service, the state's institutional history, and specialized categories.

From the first gold rush, fraternal organizations brought people together and strengthened communities. Various sections, and sometimes entire cemeteries, dedicated to fraternal organizations reveal much about a community's character and social dynamic. Chapters of the Ancient Free and Accepted Masons formed in Montana with the very beginning of its settlement history in the mid-1860s and were entwined with vigilante activities. The Masonic square and compass emblem appears on the earliest graves including that of William Bell, discussed previously, who died in 1862. Communities with substantial membership sometimes had separate Masonic cemeteries. The Masonic

Cemetery at Twin Bridges in Madison County, for example, was active from 1901 until its last burial in 1973. Like so many other small cemeteries specifically dedicated to one group, it has since suffered vandalism and has been left for grazing cattle to wander over its tombstones.

Masons are not the only group with historically maintained individual burial grounds. Only two markers remain in the abandoned Oddfellows Cemetery at Anaconda, which dates to the early 1900s. The Oddfellows Cemetery at Helena, however, is still well maintained. Roundup in Musselshell County has two cemeteries dedicated to the United Mine Workers of America representing coal miners. Tombstones frequently carry the emblems of organizations to which the deceased belonged. Besides the Masons' square and compass, other common emblems include the Oddfellows' three interlinked rings, the circle and tree stump of Woodmen of the World, the shields of the Knights of Pythias and the Knights of Columbus, branches of the military, and many others.

Anaconda's five community cemeteries are particularly representative of its working-class citizens, their cultural heritage, and trade affiliations. The fifteen thousand souls interred in Anaconda's cemeteries outnumber the living two to one.[1] In the shadow of the great Anaconda stack, the cemeteries visually reflect industrial omnipresence. The five main cemeteries together with other outlying, smaller burial grounds represent some twenty thousand souls, twice the population of today's Deer Lodge County. The expansive main cemeteries include sections, some of them gated, for various organizations including the Knights of Pythias, Brotherhood of American Yeomen, and Fraternal Order of Eagles. A spectacular monument in Upper Hill Cemetery marks the section devoted to members of the Improved Order of Red Men (IORM). This fraternal organization, founded in Baltimore in 1834, is based on temperance, patriotism and American history. The original Order of Red Men dates to the Revolutionary War and is the oldest fraternal organization in the United States. Its white members adopted rules, regalia, and rituals they perceived as Native American. The spectacular monument is a full-size tree trunk richly carved with intricate symbolism pertaining to the order. "T.O.T.E.," carved into its center, is a secret password meaning "totem of the eagle."

Most Montana communities have both nonsectarian and Catholic cemeteries, but some communities have individual burial grounds associated with other specific groups. Along Montana's Hi-line in Hill County, some fifteen miles northwest of Kremlin, the wind whips through the abandoned, hollow shell of the Milk River Valley Church of the Brethren. Nearby, a small graveyard recalls the lure of the Homestead Boom. Marked by four fence posts, burials from 1913 to 1931 chronicle Brethren parishioners who came with high hopes but ultimately left family members buried and graves untended in this very lonely place.

Lutheran cemeteries such as the still-active Melville Lutheran Cemetery in Sweet Grass County, St. Olaf Church Cemetery near Red Lodge, and the Fairview Cemetery in Richland County are reminders of Norwegian settlers and homesteaders. There are also numerous Protestant German-speaking Hutterite colonies scattered across Montana that include small cemeteries where the deceased are customarily buried in order of death and not in family plots or next to family members.

Cemeteries also reflect Montana's important African American footprint. The burial places of Black Montanans underscore the integration of these pioneers in death. Unlike the Chinese, whose burial grounds are usually set apart, African American Montanans are rarely excluded from community cemeteries. Although Montana had no Whites Only signs, Black Montanans were nevertheless excluded from restaurants, barbershops, and saloons and endured much the same discrimination as in other parts of the country. However, in Montana this ethnic group was neither segregated in schools after 1882, nor in neighborhoods, nor were Blacks excluded from the mainstream population in death. Water company owner Sarah Bickford and teamster/rancher Jack Taylor, for example, have fine, prominent granite tombstones in the center of Virginia City's Hillside Cemetery. John White, Kalispell's beloved custodian, who rang the Central School bell for nearly forty years, is buried in the Conrad Memorial Cemetery, and Havre's longtime restauranteur Alice "Ma Plaz" Pleasant is interred at the Calvary Cemetery.

There are hundreds of tribal cemeteries, small family burial grounds, and single burials on every reservation that reflect Montana's strong Native American heritage. Reservation cemeteries are often adjacent to Catholic churches. The Jocko Agency Cemetery on the Flathead Reservation, for example, sits next to St. John Berchmans Catholic Church southeast of Arlee in Lake County. The Blackfeet Reservation in Glacier County has some forty-four cemeteries, many of them small family burial grounds with three or fewer graves. The Sacred Heart Catholic Church, on the edge of the Fort Belknap Reservation near Harlem in Blaine County, established in 1924 and long abandoned, has a cemetery that remains active. Perched along U.S. Route 2 on a windswept hilltop, the pink Mission-style church is the focal point. However, the lovely adjoining Sacred Heart Catholic Cemetery, with its many personal tributes, is well worth a visit.[2]

There are a few other types of cemeteries and/or sections therein that merit individual discussion. These include the burial places of Chinese, Japanese, Jews, and the immigrant coal mining families who came to Carbon County. Chinese, Japanese, and Jews are significant because of their contributions to early settlement and because these ethno-cultural groups made significant contributions to many Montana communities. The National Register–listed cemeteries of Gebo and Bearceek in Carbon County are especially distinctive because of their cultural features. Likewise, military cemeteries, especially Montana's Custer National Cemetery, are important pieces of the Montana mosaic. Finally, a unique section of Bozeman's expansive Sunset Hills Cemetery includes the final resting places of bodies used for scientific research.

The Overseas Chinese

When the first hopeful miners swarmed across the Continental Divide to the Grasshopper diggings in 1862, Chinese miners were probably part of this initial population wave. By the later 1860s, substantial numbers of Chinese miners were among the many ethno-cultural groups to seek their fortunes in Montana.

"Overseas Chinese," beginning with the California gold rush in 1848, came to the American West primarily from Guangdong

Province where civil war, famine, and over population created dire circumstances. American gold rushes, and a bit later, the building of the railroads, provided opportunity and potential aid to families in China. Most Chinese sojourners never intended to stay in the United States. Language, customs, and sometimes city ordinances bound this almost exclusively male population together. By 1870, 10 percent of Montana's territorial population was Chinese. After passage of the 1882 federal Chinese Exclusion Act, no Chinese laborers or unskilled workers were allowed to enter the United States. While a few professional service providers and their families did settle in Montana, the Chinese population significantly diminished. Further, Montana's anti-miscegenation law—on the books from 1909 until its repeal in 1953—prevented African Americans and Asians from and marrying whites. Miners and other unskilled Chinese workers who arrived in the United States before 1882 either returned home or died here on foreign soil.[3]

Working and social conditions for the Chinese in Montana and elsewhere were harsh. Some Chinese came as individuals, but Chinese companies brought many workers to the United States under contract before the 1882 exclusion. A benefit for those who came under contract was the promise to return the person's bones to China should he die away from his homeland. It was an important incentive. If a person died on foreign soil and had no family to care for his grave, his spirit could not rest. Nineteenth-century Chinese burials were therefore oftentimes meant to be temporary. After a customary length of time, the remains were exhumed. The process varied, but one such mass exhumation, described in the *Helena Daily Independent* in 1881, details the recovery of the remains of ten individuals who had been buried for a decade or more:

> In such cases the coffins or boxes . . . are generally rotted way and it is not the easiest task to gather the bones together. . . . They turn out a lot of Chinese placer miners in the graves and these fellows go to work as if mining for gold and by digging up the earth and panning it, every bone even the carpus, meta-

carpus and tarsus bones, which are very small, are found. They are washed and spread out to dry, after which they are sacked for shipment.[4]

Archaeologists at German Gulch in Silver Bow County discovered a mysterious charcoal kiln, or oven, of local rock fashioned in a two-meter circle with an entryway and a vent. A newspaper article of 1874 offers a possible explanation:

> The Heathen element of German gulch . . . one day last week cremated six of their deceased countrymen. . . . The process is this: The dead are disinterred, the flesh scraped from the bones and these are placed in a crucible and reduced to ashes, which in this instance are to be packed in tin boxes, each box of ashes separate, and sent to the Flowery Kingdom for a final interment.[5]

The empty casket of Lee Foo Lim, discussed in a previous chapter, is one such example of repatriation. But this custom could not always be observed even in the nineteenth century and after that, repatriation was rare. Chinese sections in cemeteries at Missoula, Philipsburg, Butte, Helena, and elsewhere include historic graves that have not been disturbed. The remains of only some dozen of the more than two hundred individuals buried in China Row at Helena's Forestvale Cemetery were exhumed and returned to China. To the dismay of Helena's surviving Chinese community, China Row—outside the tended boundaries of the cemetery proper—was not included when the fence enclosed the cemetery in 1988. Cemetery officials considered it an inactive section.[6]

Chinese sections at the Butte and Helena cemeteries and the cemetery at Philipsburg preserve remnants of funerary burners characteristic of larger Chinese burial grounds. It was customary to burn various items at the site of the burial, as described during the funeral of Lo Kon:

> About twenty Chinamen followed the remains to the cemetery. . . . The coffin was decorated with bunting, peacock feathers and Chinese ornaments. When the coffin was taken from the hearse it was placed over the grave, as usual, where it remained

25. Chinese customs required burning the clothing of the deceased and other items. The funerary burner in the Chinese section at Butte's Mount Moriah Cemetery is Montana's only known surviving example. Photograph by author.

for about half an hour, during which time numerous candles were lighted around the grave and a quantity of nuts, candies, fruits, roast chicken and other delicacies were strewn in the bottom of the grave. In the meantime all the dead man's clothing is being burnt up, together with everything used about him after death. Finally the coffin is lowered into the grave and as soon as it is covered with dirt the Chinese throw everything that will not burn such as dishes, knives and forks, tin pans, whisky bottles etc. They then make a final salute and depart.[7]

The burner at Forestvale is little more than a pile of bricks, but that at Mount Moriah survives intact. Scattered artifacts and pottery sherds in all three cemeteries reveal offerings of food to the dead.

Many of the miners at Alder Gulch were under company contract and likely the remains of most who died there were returned to China. Legend has it that Virginia City's Chinese cemetery lies today beneath the city dump. The 1895 funeral of Wing Dot includes a rare mention of burial in the "Chinese Cemetery."[8] The location, however, is speculative and not all Chinese were buried there. Ah Tong's death in 1865 precipitated the first Chinese funeral in Virginia City and is described in some detail. He was buried on Boot Hill, i.e., "Cemetery Hill." There is no evidence that his remains were later exhumed. The use of red in association with death is here noted:

> The body was carried to its resting place on Cemetery Hill, in Monte's hearse, and accompanied by six Chinamen. . . . . Arrived at the grave, the coffin was interred in American fashion, but the head was reversed. Each Chinaman threw a little earth on the coffin. . . . The head-board with appropriate hieroglyphics [was placed]. Brandy and cigars were handed round to the spectators and officials. The old clothes of the deceased were piled up for burning in a fine red blanket.[9]

On the cusp of the 1882 Chinese Exclusion Act, Northern Pacific Railway president Henry Villard hired thousands of Chinese laborers, most under company contracts, to help lay the tracks across the Northwest in the early 1880s. The work was dangerous, and hundreds of Chinese died from blasting accidents, train collisions, and scurvy:

> There are probably 1,000 Chinese, who worked for the railroad company, buried between Spokane Falls and Helena. They were buried in shallow graves, and in various places the coffins are visible. Verily the road was built with Chinaman's bones.[10]

"Bone collectors" made regular sweeps through the railroad camps, and shallow graves along the railroad grade facilitated this work. Not all remains were recovered. Chinese graves, some with remains removed, have been discovered in the Noxon area near the Clark Fork River in Sanders County, along the railroad line and near the Northern Pacific depot. In the 1950s, Noxon residents removed bodies from a grove of Cottonwood trees near the depot and reburied them in the city cemetery.[11]

While many Chinese suffered harsh treatment and discrimination, Dr. Huie Pock illustrates the enduring respect that one individual earned from his western peers. The venerable doctor practiced in Butte from 1895 to his death in 1927, establishing an enviable reputation. He manufactured banana-leaf poultices that he sold by mail and cured copper king William A. Clark's daughter of a bleeding ulcer when other doctors could not. During the 1918 Spanish flu epidemic that devastated Butte, Dr. Pock's skilled use of herbal medicine helped many patients convalesce.[12]

In 1923, when Dr. Pock's wife died of botulism after eating from a tainted can, he could not save her. Her body was placed in storage at a local funeral home, awaiting return to China. When Dr. Pock himself died in 1927, he left money and instructions for his son to ship his parents back to China for burial. The son, however, squandered the money. Meanwhile, the Pocks were kept in storage in a Butte mortuary until 1953 when a lawsuit compelled the son to bury his parents. They were finally buried in unmarked graves in Mount Moriah's Chinese section. In 2007, Butte doctors paid for Dr. and Mrs. Pock's tombstone. His epitaph reads: Respected Physician.[13]

Japanese Casualties

After the Chinese Exclusion Act prohibited importing Chinese labor, the Great Northern Railway and other industries appealed to Japan for workers. Many came to the United States under contract with Japanese companies. Most of these workers, like the Chinese before them, came without their families and sent money home. The Great Northern Railway was a major employer as the tracks crept across Montana in the early 1890s. The transcontinental line, from St. Paul to Seattle, was completed in 1893, but there was still plenty of work. In the early twentieth century, many Japanese crews laid the tracks of the Milwaukee Road across Montana and worked for the various railroad companies when the lines were refurbished. Hundreds of Japanese "bandy dancers," section hands who maintained the tracks, worked in communities wherever there was rail service. Some two thousand Japanese worked for the railroad and other industries in Missoula. As it had been for the Chinese, the work was brutal. Accidents and disease took many men and Montana's cold winters were hard on those from a warmer climate.

26. Tombstones in Hillcrest Cemetery at Deer Lodge document Japanese residents, many of whom came to refurbish and maintain railroad lines. Photograph by author.

In 1903, the Northern Pacific purchased two blocks with four hundred plots in the Missoula City Cemetery for the reburial of Japanese railroad workers in Sanders County. The bodies of one hundred mostly unidentified Japanese were exhumed at Paradise and reinterred in Missoula. Four hundred others, many of whom died of influenza, were removed from shallow graves along the railroad beds at Thompson Falls and Plains and reinterred at Missoula. The Northern Pacific set stones marking these graves in Japanese script with names, dates, and town of origin, if known. Following Japanese custom, visitors to this section burn incense to cleanse the area and leave white carnations as a symbol of cleansing and peace.[14]

Other communities also include Japanese interments. Harlowton in Wheatland County once had a Japanese community of two hundred. Only two headstones remain in the community's old cemetery adjacent to the Jawbone Creek Country Club's golf course. One of them, dated 1917, is in Japanese.[15] Another group is in Hillcrest Cemetery in Deer Lodge, Powell County, where a row of some twenty tombstones document Japanese residents.

Jewish Pioneers

Jews, many of them immigrants from poor villages in Poland, Germany, Austria, and Prussia, were among the fortune seekers who came to Montana during the gold rush. Some came to prospect, but it was especially in the roles of merchant and provider that these enterprising men prospered. They set up some of the first shops at Bannack and then at Virginia City. The gold rush provided a tremendous steppingstone to move on to entrepreneurial pursuits and gain economic stability and civic status in a single generation.[16]

By the mid-1860s, Jews were active community participants. During the territory's turbulent first years, the vigilantes that organized included at least two Jews. Ben Ezekiel, born to Jewish parents in England, served as one of two "sentries" who guarded George Ives during his dramatic Nevada City trial and before his public hanging in 1863. Ezekiel went on to serve in public office and law enforcement, as chief clerk of the House during several legislative sessions, and as a territorial legislator from Madison County. Samuel Schwab, born in Rimpar, Bavaria, rode the first stage from Salt Lake City to Bannack bringing essential goods to peddle to the miners. He, like Ezekiel, was also active in the early community and listed in the roster as a vigilante.[17]

Virginia City's Jewish community was large enough to form a Hebrew Benevolent Society, a necessary first step in establishing a formal burial ground. No records are extant for the Virginia City organization; however, the town's first plat map, drawn in 1868, includes a proposed Hebrew Cemetery.[18] Even so, the cemetery and two other structures advertised on the map—a capitol building and an elegant Episcopal church—never came to fruition. As gold was discovered at Last Chance Gulch in 1864 and placer gold dwindled at Alder Gulch, by 1866, most residents had moved on to the new boomtown of Helena. There are no recorded deaths of Virginia City Jews at any time—except for that of Solomon Content in 1870—and the Benevolent Society never purchased the land for the cemetery.

Former Virginia City Jews and others organized a Hebrew Benevolent Society at Helena in 1866 and established the National Register–listed Home of Peace Cemetery in 1867. It was Montana's first Jewish cemetery. Until 1891 Helena Jews had no synagogue and no rabbi as was often the case in early western communities. The Benevolent Society bound the group together. Members, as in Hebrew benevolent societies in other places across the West, maintained Jewish holidays; conducted prescribed rituals; offered financial assistance to the needy; saw to the medical care and burial of victims of accidents, disease, and violence; and encouraged charitable acts.

The original 1867 wrought iron fence, extending well beyond the cemetery's current boundaries, illustrates the intended expansion of the Home of Peace. The first two burials, those of Emanuel Blum, who died on May 5, 1865, and H. L. Schlessinger, who died in October 1867, were reinterments from Helena's City Cemetery.[19] Jews from other communities without Hebrew burial grounds were buried at the Home of Peace. That included Solomon Content of Virginia City mentioned previously and B. Wolff of Deer Lodge who died in 1872. Among the 240 recorded burials, tombstones mark 204 graves.[20] Former Virginia City vigilantes Ben Ezekiel and Samuel Schwab are also buried there.

The original wagon road, lined with trees planted circa 1910, runs the length of the grounds. The cemetery was planned in a simple square in 1867, with landscaping added later. Architecturally, the plan was later modified and is unusual in that close-knit families cluster together in death as they did in life, as in a village. Stone curbing binds households together and brick walkways separate family units. The oldest tombstone, that of Hattie Jacobs, is badly weathered and spalled; it dates to 1870. The first twelve graves lie unmarked at an odd angle, outside the modern fence to the north.

Among the first burials is that of Mary Goldman whose death in 1869 demonstrates how the society grappled with questions of religious propriety without counsel of a rabbi. The youngster had died of seizures. Mary was not Jewish by birth but by adoption and choice. Her age is unknown, but she is described as "in her girlhood years." Her intent was to convert to Judaism, but she was too young to have accomplished this. Her place of burial therefore was a serious question given the rule that only Jews could be buried in the Home of Peace. The lack of a rabbi to resolve the question is presumably why there was more than a week's delay in her burial. Finally, the society determined that she was young and innocent, and her intent was enough to allow her burial there. Hers was the largest funeral in Montana to date. Four horses draped and plumed in black drew the hearse. Thirty single and double carriages and buggies, the teams of many of them also plumed in black, followed. Forty horsemen drew up the rear.[21]

Into the early twentieth century, marriages between Jews and gentiles among Helena families became more frequent as the second generation came of age. Children moved away to pursue job opportunities, and the once stringent cemetery rules began to relax. In 1916, the Board of Trustees agreed to emend the article of the constitution stating that only persons of the Jewish faith could be buried in the cemetery. Thereafter, the rules not only allowed gentile spouses and their unmarried children burial in the cemetery, but also non-Jewish funerals.[22]

The Home of Peace is the oldest Jewish cemetery in Montana and Helena's oldest active cemetery. Other Jewish cemeteries include Butte's B'nai Israel Cemetery, formally established in 1885. Its earliest recorded grave, that of David Mendelsohn, dates to 1880. There are between five hundred and one thousand graves in this cemetery. A small Jewish cemetery located south of Great Falls dates to the early nineteenth century and contains fewer than twelve graves. In 1916 the cemetery merged with the Great Falls Hebrew Association. Although its last burial was in 1940, some Great Falls residents currently plan to be buried there. Until 1918, Jews who died in Billings were buried in the B'nai Israel Cemetery at Butte, but this changed during the Spanish flu epidemic. Butte was overwhelmed with deaths and could only bury its own local victims. The Congregation Beth Aaron established the Beth Aaron Cemetery in Billings at that time. Beth Aaron has ninety-five graves and 225 additional plots.

Visitors to Jewish cemeteries do not leave flower offerings. Rather, it is common to see a stone or stones placed upon a tombstone. This may go back to the practice of using stones to mark a person's grave. There are several explanations for this practice, but one idea is that leaving flowers was a pagan practice. Also, stones do not wither, rather they show that someone visited, and that the deceased is in the visitor's thoughts. Although the stones may seem in disarray, it is disrespectful to remove another's stone. The more stones a grave has, the more respected was the person.

Coal Mining at Bearcreek and Gebo

Coal needed to fuel the steam engines of the Northern Pacific and the copper smelters at Butte and Anaconda brought miners to Carbon County, where rich deposits lay. The coal-mining communities of Gebo, near present-day Fromberg, and Bearcreek, near Red Lodge, once thrived. Miners came from diverse places but today, the cemeteries of these two communities, both listed in the National Register, tell the tale of boom and bust.

The cemetery at Gebo is a simple square of several acres with a loop drive around it. The location affords a scenic panoramic view of the Clarks Fork Valley. It is the last intact remnant of Gebo, a town that supported as many as a thousand people in the early twentieth century. Founded in 1899, its prosperity was short-lived. By 1904, miners found easier diggings and higher quality seams elsewhere. By 1906, most residents had relocated to Fromberg and by the time the local mine closed in 1912, only a handful of diehards remained.[23]

Rattlesnakes favor the habitat where cactus and sagebrush have grown over many of the several hundred graves, but here and there a tenacious lilac or a purple iris, planted by a grieving family long ago, bloom among the lambs and cherubs. These carved symbols of innocence recall the real tragedy of Gebo: that some sixty of the one hundred twenty-nine marked graves are those of children under the age of two. Distinctive features are three wrought iron crosses that mark the graves of German-Russian Catholics from the Black Sea region of Russia. Families continued to use the cemetery in the 1930s and there are still occasional burials.[24]

The small, four-acre cemetery at Bearcreek has historic significance for several reasons. The coal-mining community was home to many cultural groups including Croatian, Montenegrin, Slavic, Italian, Scottish, German, Finnish, French, and English. The names on the tombstones, many of them in Cyrillic, reflect this ethnic diversity. There are fewer than five hundred burials, but one hundred seven of them are children and twenty-two are victims of Montana's greatest coal-mining disaster. The deaths of so many children and the Smith Mine disaster especially underscore the dangers and harshness of life among Bearcreek villagers.[25]

The cemetery opened in 1909, laid out with a central circle into which roads merge from the north, south, east, and west. No trees or plantings soften the barren landscape. A sculptured angel stands out among the other more modest markers, looking over the grave of nineteen-year-old Sidonie Cenis who died in 1911. Heavy white concrete fence posts outline the family plot. Bearcreek's first burial was that of six-year-old Helen Markovich. The simple epitaph her grieving parents had carved into her headstone, now broken into pieces, reads simply: At Rest.

By World War II, small-time coal mining was on the downswing at Bearcreek. The Smith Mine probably would have soon closed, but an underground methane gas explosion on February 27, 1943, hastened its demise. The explosion and poisonous gas killed seventy-four men and one rescuer. The mine never reopened, and most surviving residents left Bearcreek. Family plots in the small wind-swept burial ground were left untended. A large granite monument, erected in 1947 by the United Mine Workers of America, lists the names of those killed and memorializes Montana's worst coal mining disaster. The village, however, did not entirely die. A few residents still call Bearcreek home.

Remembering Veterans

The creation of national cemeteries was one legacy of the Civil War. There were an astounding number of casualties and families often did not know if their loved one lived or died. The public demanded that the government assume the responsibility of identification and burial of war dead. In 1861, the Quartermaster General took charge of registering and burying casualties. By 1862, there were fourteen national cemeteries. The National Cemetery Act of 1867 provided funds for purchase of lands, set forth appropriate regulations, and assured that every burial plot in a national cemetery be equal. The deceased are never placed according to rank, assuring that each soldier's service is equally significant.[26]

The Custer National Cemetery near Hardin was designated in 1886 at the site of the Battle of the Little Bighorn. Like many national cemeteries, the Custer cemetery was created on a battlefield where there were already burials. It is part of a National Historic Monument, administered by the National Park Service. Burial reservations at the Custer National Cemetery closed in 1978.

The Department of Veterans Affairs funds Montana's two other national cemeteries: Fort Missoula Post Cemetery at Missoula and the Yellowstone National Cemetery at Laurel. The National Register–listed Fort Missoula Post Cemetery opened in 1878 and is now closed to burial reservations.

Montana has four state-funded veterans' cemeteries at Miles City, Missoula, Crow Agency, and Helena. Eligibility for burial in these cemeteries extends to spouses and dependent children and others in special situations. Many veterans are also buried in the Montana Veterans' Home Cemetery at Columbia Falls.

27. Burials in the Custer National Cemetery include military personal and their families, many of whom have been moved from historic cemeteries attached to Montana's military posts. Photograph by author.

In addition, numerous Montana cemeteries include a section reserved for veterans.

Visitors to veterans' graves might notice coins left on their tombstones. The custom of leaving items for the dead is nothing new. Roman soldiers placed a coin in the mouth of a deceased comrade to ensure passage across the River Styx to the afterlife. But the custom among American military seems to be recent, dating to 2009. A penny thanks the veteran for his or her service, a nickel means the visitor trained at boot camp with the deceased, and a dime means the visitor served with him or her. A quarter means the visitor was with the person when he or she passed away. Cemetery groundskeepers periodically collect the change and it usually goes toward maintaining the grounds.[27]

Institutional Cemeteries

The Montana Territory faced the same dilemma that eventually confronts every settled place: what to do about orphans, the indigent sick and elderly, and the mentally ill. Early on, Catholic sisters took care of much of this marginalized population. But as the territory became better organized, institutions began to take responsibility. Montana has many cemeteries and/or sections in larger burial grounds dedicated to institutions.

The territorial prison at Deer Lodge in present-day Powell County was the first institution in Montana to set aside a burial site. The prison operated as a federal facility until statehood in 1889. Founded in 1870, Deer Lodge accepted its first inmates in 1871. The prison was a terrible place, freezing in winter and sweltering in the summer. During territorial days, there was no wall around it or outside security, and prisoners therefore could never leave their cells. Inmates used buckets to relieve themselves. Filth and infestations along with the overpowering stench produced unhealthy conditions even for those with the strongest constitutions. Sub-standard conditions persisted until the prison closed in 1979. To die in such a place was the ultimate degradation.

A section of Hillcrest Cemetery at Deer Lodge was set aside for prisoners in 1870. Large, natural stones intermixed with a few headstones neatly delineate the many rows of graves. The site leaves a painful impression of so many lives lost to ignominy. Squares of spalled concrete mark the first and earliest rows of graves at the back. A few are stamped with names and dates, but most are unreadable or lack identification. The first recorded burial is that of H. B. Fanning who died in 1872.[28] Fanning was serving a six-year sentence for stealing $400 in gold. He was but the first of many after him who died of consumption in the prison's dark, dank cells. Fanning's grave is unmarked. A wooden sign at the corner of the cemetery reads: "Lord Remember Me."

Children's graves are always heartbreaking, but the cemetery at Twin Bridges in Madison County includes a wrenching memorial to the many children who died at the Montana State Orphans Home, later renamed the Montana State Children's Center. The vacant campus, in use from 1894 to 1984, is no less forbidding now than it was for nearly a century when hundreds of cast-off and abandoned children shed their childhoods and their youth there. Many children died while in the state's care. Only a few of the children's graves in the Twin Bridges Cemetery have tomb-stones. A memorial plaque with more than ninety names has a bittersweet epitaph: "Rest in Peace Little Angels: God's Orphans Now."

Similarly, a section in Forestvale Cemetery at Helena was reserved for the Montana Children's Home and Hospital, origi-nally a nonsectarian orphanage whose mission was to place chil-dren for adoption, countering the Catholic St. Joseph's Orphan's Home, also in Helena, and the state facility at Twin Bridges. Some twenty-two children from the Montana Children's Home were buried there between 1917 and 1932. In the 1930s, with a bequest from Louis Shodair of Butte, Shodair Children's Hospital became part of the children's home and eventually replaced it entirely. Today, Shodair is the only Montana member of the national Chil-dren's Miracle Network. The Forestvale section includes only a few individual markers; one large inclusive headstone reads sim-ply: "Resting Place."

Most Montana counties had "poor farms" where indigent per-sons could go for housing, food, and medical care. The farms were self-sustaining, and the "inmates" worked according to their abilities. County or poor farm cemeteries were usually attached to these institutions. In urban areas, poor farm cemeteries have often been developed and built over or forgotten.

The Lewis and Clark County Poor Farm and the Butte-Silver Bow Poor Farm were the state's largest facilities for the indigent. Both cemeteries survive although neither has marked graves nor memorials. Located on the outskirts of Helena at the end of Cooney Drive, the Lewis and Clark County poor farm complex is a National Register–listed district. The poor farm cemetery, in a field northwest of the old county hospital and outbuildings, holds perhaps three hundred fifty unmarked graves from the 1880s to the 1920s.[29]

The Silver Bow County Poor Farm's remaining building, also National Register listed, is now the National Center for Appro-priate Technology (NCAT), on Continental Drive. The poor farm cemetery lies to the northeast on Continental Drive. It was in use from the late nineteenth century until 1912 when other Butte cemeteries became the usual burial grounds for indigents. Unlike that in Lewis and Clark County, Butte's poor farm cemetery is well defined. In 1930, concrete slabs were laid around its one-acre perimeter. A century of neglect has taken its toll on these forgotten places where deaths of "throw away" people were unceremonious and graves undecorated.[30]

Yellowstone County's poor farm in Billings, built in 1912 and demolished in 1966, sat on a bench overlooking the Yellowstone River. Riverside Cemetery is down the road to the northeast on a triangular corner of the farm property. It is well-marked and fenced. Riverside may be the best preserved of Montana's poor farm cemeteries because Yellowstone County continues to use it. The earliest recorded burial is 1911, but most of the six hundred-plus interments date from the mid-twentieth century to the present.[31]

Some communities do choose to remember the poor, sick, elderly, and cast-off humanity. In Missoula, Rattlesnake Elementary School is built over the site of the Missoula County Poor Farm and its cemetery; perhaps as many as a thousand graves still lie beneath.[32] In 1992, the school dedicated a memorial, noting the cultural diversity of those who died and were buried at the county home between 1888 and 1930. The marker reads in part: "Through this memorial we hope you will remember the individual man, woman and child, the poor, the forgotten."

Montana's largest institutional cemetery is that of the Montana State Hospital at Warm Springs where there are some twenty-four hundred interments, perhaps hundreds more. The hospital, founded in 1877 as the "territorial asylum for the insane," became a state institution in 1912. It remains the only public psychiatric facility in the state. The adjacent historic cemetery dates from the founding of the hospital to the 1960s. There are no marked graves of the earliest period and very few tombstones of the later decades. Many are simply labeled with unreadable rusted metal tags. The vast cemetery is all but abandoned and visitation restricted. Hundreds of graves are unmarked, lying in untended fields. Decayed and warped wooden signs with peeling paint note the various sections.

28. Section markers are the only indication that there are burials in the vast institutional cemetery at Warm Springs. Photograph by author.

One Final Gift

The Montana Body Donation Program, in partnership with the Washington, Wyoming, Alaska, Montana, and Idaho (WWAMI) Medical Education Program, provides essential hands-on experience that students in centuries past could rarely gain. Cadavers were difficult to obtain because of the belief that dissection, or harming a body, prevented entry into the afterlife. The bodies of executed criminals, or freshly buried cadavers that medical students were notorious for stealing, were the usual sources. Anatomy classes were almost always held in an amphitheater setting with the professor doing the dissection and the students observing. In the United States, the Crimes Act of 1790 that permitted the death sentence of murderers also allowed the punitive dissection of their bodies as further insult. Even so, it was rare for a student to participate in the process. Today as in centuries past, textbooks, lectures, and demonstrations are no substitute for the human body.

Some Montana residents choose to make the extraordinary gift that goes to educate student doctors, nurses, and physical therapists in anatomy classes at The University of Montana, Montana State University, and in related medical and health profession schools across the Northwest. Faculty and students of participating institutions are enormously grateful and treat the body with utmost respect. Donor anonymity is strictly protected. Students view the donor as their first patient and best teacher.[33] Some programs even hold memorial services for the donor.

After use of the body during a period of one to five years, the ashes can be returned to the family or the ashes or the body can be buried at Sunset Hills Cemetery in Bozeman. An obscure section of several rows of flat gravestones mark the remains of those who were so generous. The inscription is entirely anonymous and simply reads: "For the Advancement of Medical Education." A date below the inscription reflects not the date of the donor's death, but rather the date that the body no longer served an educational purpose.

TEN

Homage to the Dead

Butte Warehouse Explosion

From the earliest ages, preparation for interment has involved ritual and ceremony. Funerals, whether private and simple or elaborate and public, not only honor the dead but also help those who mourn the passing. Montana has had some spectacular public events paying homage to the dead. One of these events came in 1895 after the great warehouse explosion in Butte. It was one of Montana's worst disasters and claimed at least fifty-seven lives including many civilians, most of the city's fire department, and three of its best horses. Because of Butte's transient population in the nineteenth century and the violence of the several explosions that reduced humans to atoms, the exact number of lives lost can never be known for certain.

The explosions occurred on the evening of January 15, 1895, as Butte firemen answered the alarm of a small fire at the Royal Milling Company in Butte's warehouse district. No one knew that tons of dynamite were illegally stored in the Kenyon-Connell Commercial Company and Butte Hardware warehouses. The fire touched off a series of explosions. The first and second blasts sent iron pipes, metal sheets, and debris across a wide area, and glass from shattered windows littered sidewalks all over Butte: "Blood and brains were splattered all about. Here were arms and legs scattered around, and there were pieces of flesh and entrails. It was sickening."[1]

Newspapers across the nation published accounts of the explosions. There were grisly, graphic eyewitness descriptions:

> One man says he picked up a head with part of a shoulder attached to it just thrown at his feet and he fancied there was a dying gasp. As long as he lives he will never forget the frozen horror in the eyes of the bodyless head, made lurid by the fearful flame.[2]

A public funeral for thirty of the victims, including the thirteen firefighters, drew far-flung mourners. Following services at various churches, hearses began lining up in front of city hall. A long procession took place even as remains were still being pulled from the ruins. Governor John E. Rickards, his staff, and firefighters from across the state walked behind the many hearses and wagons bearing multiple caskets. Carriages and buggies of dozens of prominent citizens followed. The procession of two thousand started out as the bell of city hall began to toll. It moved to the beat of muffled drums as the Musicians Union and the Silver Bow bands played the dirge.[3]

Throughout the crowd there was graphic evidence of widespread injuries. Onlookers stood with battered faces and bandaged heads and limbs. The column made its way to Mount Moriah Cemetery. At the gate, troops moved to one side and presented arms as the procession moved into the cemetery and victims were committed to their respective waiting graves. Chief Angus Cameron, identified only by his belt buckle along with three others blown to bits, were in a single casket and consigned to one grave. The procession moved on to St. Patrick's Catholic Cemetery where others were then buried.[4]

Although a coroner's inquest found the Kenyon-Connell and Butte Hardware companies guilty of criminal negligence, a judge found that the employees and owners were not responsible, and victims' families were never awarded compensation. The one positive outcome came in 1899 with the passage of House Bill 17, which provided the first disability and retirement fund for Montana firemen.[5]

Homage to the Dead

One of the most dignified funerals Montana has witnessed was that of Chief Plenty Coups on March 9, 1932. Plenty Coups was the last great leader of the Crow people and an eloquent spokesperson, a friend to all, and a statesman with a generous heart. He served as a bridge to his people between a vanished lifestyle and reservation life. In 1921, he walked with the greatest men of his time, representing all American Indians at the dedication of the Tomb of the Unknown Soldier at Arlington Cemetery in Washington DC. He lay a feathered headdress and coups stick on the marble sarcophagus drawing more press than any of the dignitaries attending. He later gave his forty-acre homestead to the United States as a public park to show enduring friendship between Crow and white.

Plenty Coups died at his home in Pryor on March 4, 1932, at eighty-five. The Right Reverend Edwin V. O'Hara, bishop of the Diocese of Great Falls, performed the solemn rites of the Catholic church at his funeral. It was a simple yet profound event. Despite bitter cold and blowing snow, both Indians and whites thronged from far distances to pay tribute. Even the U.S. Congress in Washington paused in respect.[6] Six pallbearers on horseback, followed by the casket on a horse-drawn sleigh, led the long procession. Wagons, cars, a uniformed military contingent, and people on foot wound from St. Charles Chapel to the simple family burial ground across the meadow and below the chief's home. A white seagull soared majestically overhead as the procession began.[7]

After the graveside committal service, the Indian superintendent spoke, his son played taps, and Reverend John H. Frost, Baptist missionary at Pryor who had long served as Plenty Coups's interpreter, gave a brief eulogy. As they prepared to lower the casket, covered with Plenty Coups's own banner of blue with the Crow emblem, his war bonnet was brought forward and placed with him. The Crow spoke of their chief's accomplishments, then sang Plenty Coups's own song, which he had sung many times, describing his exploits. After this, the song would never be sung again. Death chants began as mourners took turns dropping clods of earth into the grave, symbolizing acceptance and

29. Two pallbearers, wearing feather headdresses and blankets, stand with the casket of Plenty Coups during his funeral. Montana Historical Society Photograph Archives. Photograph by Earl E. Snook, 1932.

finality. Crow men passed the pipe as a group of women, heads bowed, sat quietly on a blanket in the snow. Thus "the greatest modern figure of American Indian life" was put to final rest.[8]

Luther Sage "Yellowstone" Kelly

Billings witnessed the spectacular funeral of Luther Sage "Yellowstone" Kelly on June 26, 1929. Kelly had died at seventy-nine in California the previous December and requested burial in Montana. The Billings Commercial Club chose his grave site overlooking the Yellowstone Valley. Born in Geneva, New York on July 27, 1849, Kelly spent his earliest career in Montana, where he proved himself as a hunter, trapper, and explorer. Admired as literate, courteous, and of fine character, he was also a distinguished veteran of both the Civil War and the Spanish American War. Kelly could have been buried at Arlington National Cemetery, but maintained at the end, "My body will rest better in Montana." The funeral cortege made its way through downtown Billings to the monotonous beat of muffled drums. A second procession followed along the rimrocks to the grave site. Veterans of earlier wars, state officials, a firing squad, and a horse with reversed boots led the way according to strict military protocol. The body lay in a flag-draped casket. A horse-drawn wagon carried the remains of a man who symbolized to many the ideal frontiersman.[9] Kelly's grave site is included in the scenic National Register–listed Black Otter Trail Historic District.

Charles M. Russell

On October 27, 1926, flags in Great Falls flew at half-staff, district court adjourned, county offices closed, and schools were dismissed for the funeral of Montana's own cowboy artist, Charles M. Russell. Charlie, who died at his home in Great Falls of a sudden heart attack, always maintained that he belonged to no church but respected all of them and counted priests and ministers from many denominations among his friends. The open casket first lay at the Russells' home, then at the Episcopal Church of the Incarnation where hundreds filed past.[10]

Charlie had requested that when the time came, he be taken to his grave by horses. That request was honored. Thousands lined the streets and children by the hundreds stood in formation. A team of black horses drew the antique, glass-sided hearse, with the coffin visible inside, as it threaded its way through Great Falls to Highland Cemetery. An old-time stage driver, who had ridden the range with a young Charlie, drove the team. Three horses followed, equipped as if for range-riding the way Charlie knew it in his youth. Two horses carried riders, but the third was Charlie's own horse, with his saddle empty.[11]

The afternoon seemed surreal., All the colors of Charlie's famous palette splashed across the landscape, augmented when a rainbow, highly unusual for October, showed itself across the sky like brush strokes on a Russell canvas. As the procession of one hundred cars made its way behind the hearse, another hundred waited at the cemetery. Banks of floral tributes artistically fashioned in the shapes of lariats and Charlie's signature buffalo skull covered the grave site and scented the air. Most intricate was a replica of Charlie's saddle, arranged entirely in flowers, from his good friend, Will Rogers. A large natural boul-

30. A horse-drawn hearse carries the body of Charles M. Russell through a crowded residential street in Great Falls. Pearl Thompson, photographer, 1926. Montana Historical Society Photograph Archives.

der from the West Quincy Quarry at Square Butte, inset with a simple bronze nameplate in the shape of an artist's palette, marks Charlie Russell's grave. From this vantage point in Highland Cemetery, with sweeping, panoramic views of the what is now known as Russell Country, Charlie sleeps the "Big Sleep" under his beloved Big Sky.

Commemorating Disasters

Most communities have various memorials to honor veterans or individuals, which are beyond the scope of this work. However, a few memorials pay tribute to multiple lives lost due to natural and man-made events and it would be remiss not to include these. Because of its mining birthright, two disasters are an integral part of Butte's industrial heritage: The Great Warehouse Explosion of 1895, discussed previously, and the Granite Mountain-Speculator Mine explosion in 1917. These two events left indelible marks on Butte's landscape and on its psyche.

The Granite Mountain disaster caused the deaths of more than one hundred sixty men. On June 8, 1917, a carbide lamp at the North Butte Mining Company's Speculator Mine ignited

31. A granite marker in Butte's Mountain View Cemetery commemorates the unknown dead of the 1917 Granite Mountain-Speculator Mine disaster in Butte. Photograph by Jon Axline.

frayed electrical insulation in the Granite Mountain Shaft. Fire spread, and carbon monoxide and other deadly gasses swept through the tunnels. Some died instantly, but others had time to scrawl poignant goodbye letters to their families, in the darkness, as the oxygen ran out. A brass plaque names sixty-five of the victims whose remains lie in a mass grave in Butte's Mountain View Cemetery. The granite marker, provided by the North Butte Mining Company, reads: "In Memory of the Unidentified Dead of the Granite Mountain Fire June 8, 1917."

In 1996, Butte dedicated the expansive Granite Mountain Memorial overlooking the site of the disaster. A visit to this site is visceral and unforgettable. Facsimiles of some of the men's final words fringe the monument. That site, however, is not Butte's only mass catastrophe commemoration.

Butte has numerous other memorials in addition to Granite Mountain, but until recently there had never been an effort to commemorate the devastating 1895 warehouse explosion. This event was so traumatic that for decades after, citizens reckoned time in terms of years before or after the "Big Explosion." Only the Speculator Mine disaster eclipsed it. High school students in the Butte History Club noticed the lack of recognition for this event and thought it was a serious oversight. They proposed a memorial. The community rallied around the idea. After some years in the planning, the first of several sculptures commemorating this event on the site was completed in 2019.[12]

In Carbon County, seventy-four men and one rescuer lost their lives at Bearcreek's Smith Mine in 1943, Montana's worst coal mining disaster. It left 176 children fatherless. Some died in an explosion, but most succumbed to poisonous methane gas as it seeped into the underground spaces. Miners trapped there knew they could not escape. Several had time to scrawl messages to loved ones. Walter and Johnny wrote: "Goodbye. Wifes and daughters. We died an easy death. Love from us both. Be good."

The National Register–listed mine buildings loom over the landscape, recalling the families who waited there for word of survivors. But there were none. The disaster prompted changes in mining safety. A roadside marker at the mine recounts the story and a granite monument at the Bearcreek Cemetery lists the names of those who perished.

Not all Montana disasters have been caused by humans. On August 5, 1949, fifteen smokejumpers from Missoula responded to a lightning-sparked fire in the Gates of the Mountains Wilderness in the Helena National Forest. They parachuted into the funnel-shaped drainage and rendezvoused with a former smokejumper working as a fire guard nearby. High winds fed the fire and it was very quickly out of control trapping the men. The Mann Gulch fire and the thirteen lives it took is the subject of Norman Maclean's best seller, *Young Men and Fire*. The book provides an agonizing yet compelling account of firefighting and its human toll. The thirteen young lives lost, five thousand acres of wilderness burned, and the lessons learned about "blowup" fires continue to influence wilderness firefighting. National Register–listed Mann Gulch is inaccessible except by boat and on foot. Crosses, spread out across the rugged landscape, mark the places where each of the thirteen men fell.[13]

At the southwest corner of Gallatin County, a bronze plaque on a three-thousand-ton dolomite boulder contains the names

32. U.S. Forest Service personnel retrieve bodies from the burned
and rugged north slope of Mann Gulch, August 6, 1949. / Wikimedia
Commons contributors, https://commons.wikimedia.org/w/index.php
?title=File:Mann_Gulch_Fire,_1949._US_Forest_Service,_retrieval_of
_victim%27s_bodies.jpg&oldid=356876668.

of twenty-eight known men, women, and children who lost their
lives when the mountain came tumbling down upon them. In
the late evening of August 17, 1959, the peaceful sounds of the
Madison River lulled vacationers who packed the campgrounds.
As some two hundred fifty campers enjoyed the summer evening or slept, a 7.5-magnitude earthquake sent this boulder and
hundreds of others careening across the canyon. In the aftermath, choking dust, giant waves, and impassable roads impeded
rescuers. In the darkness, family members were separated and
injured. Nineteen campers at the Rock Creek Campground lie
buried beneath the boulders. Another nine died at other locations.[14] The disaster created Quake Lake, along Route 287 mostly
in the Gallatin National Forest, northwest of West Yellowstone.
The lake is 190 feet deep and six miles long.

The Fort Peck Dam in Valley County near Glasgow was President Franklin Roosevelt's most ambitious New Deal project.
It gave more than ten thousand workers jobs during the 1930s

depression and created Fort Peck Lake. The monumental one-hundred-million-dollar construction project began in 1933 and was not completed until 1940. Working conditions were hazardous and the weather unforgiving with record low temperatures in winter and sweltering heat in the summer. Some sixty workers died during the construction. A jagged slab of rock at the east end of the dam is inscribed with the names of eight of those who died in a disaster on September 22, 1938. A section of the dam gave way, killing one and burying seven others. Only two of the bodies were recovered. The stark slab overlooking the awe-inspiring dam is a jarring reminder that the project was not only monetarily expensive, but also cost lives as well. It reads in part, "In memory of those who lost their lives in 'The Slide' . . . forever entombed in the dam."

Memorializing Beloved Nonhumans

Many Montana communities have pet cemeteries, evidence that Montanans love their nonhuman companions and grieve when they cross the Rainbow Bridge. But sometimes animals become more than pets, cherished by their entire communities, and their deaths bring profound grief. Here are a few examples of beloved animals and how their communities have remembered them.

A sheepherder fell ill and died after several days in the hospital at Fort Benton in the summer of 1936. The sheepherder's faithful dog followed his master to the hospital and haunted the back door where a sympathetic nun saw that he was fed. When his master died, relatives asked that his remains be shipped back east, and as the casket was loaded aboard the train, the dog was right there. When the train pulled away, he tried to follow until the train was out of sight. Thereafter, every day for five and a half years through heat, rain, sleet, and snow, the dog waited for his master's return. He met every train, watching as each person stepped off onto the platform.[15]

Locals named him Shep, and his fame spread. Many tried to adopt him, but Shep would have none of that. He had formed a bond with his master and no one else could fill that void. Depot agent Tony Schanche finally persuaded Shep to come out of the winter cold and into the depot where he eventually halfway gained Shep's trust.[16] Shep's fame spread as old age crept into his joints. Arthritis left him stiff-legged, and he lost his hearing. On a wintery January morning in 1942, as the 10:17 approached the depot, Shep did not hear the whistle until the engine was nearly upon him. He turned to see the engine bearing down and at the last moment, slipped on the ice-covered tracks. Thus Shep's longtime vigil ended.

The community chose a fitting grave site, on a bluff overlooking the station, and gave Shep a fine funeral. A local minister read a poignant eulogy on man's best friend, and Boy Scouts played taps.[17] An obelisk, lit at night, marked the grave for every incoming passenger train to see until train traffic ended, and the grave fell into disrepair. Fort Benton's love for Shep never diminished. The community restored the grave site in the 1980s. In 1994, a magnificent, larger-than-life bronze likeness of Shep, with his front feet on a train rail, was dedicated to him and placed in the middle of town. The "Forever Faithful" monument commemorates Shep and the special bond between man and dog.

Other Montana dogs also live on in the state's memory. Foremost is Auditor, a matted, mangy canine who lived for some seventeen lonely years on the acrid, crusted shores of Butte's poisonous Berkeley Pit. His origin was a mystery and throughout his long life, he would periodically disappear and then show up again. His unpredictability led miners working in the area to name him Auditor. He never sought out human companions although many humans tried hard to win him over. Miners fed him and made him a little dog shanty out of scraps where he had a bed of rags, but he never spent much time there. Only occasionally did he settle in his bed at night.

Auditor's ancestry may have been Hungarian Komondor or Puli. His long, tangled dreadlocks made him look like a moving pile of rags but probably kept him warm during Montana's brutal winters. As the years closed in, the miners who fed him mixed baby aspirin into his food to ease arthritis. Once one patient miner got close enough to trim the hair that hung over Auditor's eyes. Those who knew him best claimed that beneath those

33. With one foot on a railway track, *Ever Faithful*, Bob Scriver's sculpture of Shep in Fort Benton, recalls the bond between a dog and his master. / Wikimedia Commons contributors, https://commons.wikimedia.org/w /index.php?title=File:Shep_monument_in_front_of_the_Grand_Union _Hotel,_Fort_Benton,_Montana.JPG&oldid=254229611.

dreadlocks, his eyes were beautiful. Auditor lived a long life where no other creature could. The pads of his feet somehow became accustomed to the landscape. The end came in 2003 when the elderly Auditor died peacefully in his shanty.

Loving hands spread his ashes over the Granite Mountain Mine. There are several statues around Butte commemorating Auditor. One likeness, temporarily displayed at the Butte-Silver Bow Chamber of Commerce, will eventually be relocated to the Berkeley Pit, where Auditor lived out his long life.[18]

Butte has plans to memorialize two other animals, a dog and a horse, as part of the Butte Warehouse Explosion Memorial. The dog, whose name is unknown, belonged to fireman William Copeland. The dog was with him but uninjured when Copeland died in the explosion in 1895. The big black dog followed his master's coffin to Mount Moriah Cemetery and never strayed far until his death a few weeks later. Whether he died of exposure in freezing February weather or died of a broken heart is up to interpretation. Although injured in the explosion, the one surviving horse, Jim, became a Butte legend. Artist Jim Dolan has completed a sculpture—the first of this memorial—installed in 2019. These two animals figure prominently in the planned warehouse explosion memorial.

The legacy of another dog survives in the hearts of Harlowton residents. Smoking Boomer arrived at Harlowton in 1940, riding into the railyards on a Milwaukee train. Harlowton was once the eastern terminus of the electrified Milwaukee Road and thus the end of the line. The dog was a broad-shouldered, powerful mutt who showed up with no owner. Roundhouse foreman Phil Leahy fed him and the two formed a close bond. He was a smart dog and a character. Leahy adopted him and taught him to stand on his head. He was called Smoking Boomer because he strutted along the depot platform wearing safety glasses and sporting a pipe clamped firmly between his powerful jaws. Smoking Boomer became famous for his comical antics as he greeted *The Hiawatha*, Milwaukee Road's passenger train. For nine years, he delighted travelers and was always willing to strike a pose for their cameras. When Smoking Boomer died in 1949, the town mourned his loss and furnished him with a casket and a proper funeral. Smoking Boomer was long remembered. In 2006, the City of Harlowton and community volunteers established a recreational trail. Its northern end follows the Main Line of the old Milwaukee Railroad and is officially named the Smoking Boomer Rail Trail.[19]

A memorial in an unlikely place in Dillon tells the sad story of Old Pitt. She originally belonged to John Robinson III who at one time had the largest elephant herd in captivity. From the 1880s to the 1910s, Robinson trained and traveled with his pachyderms until hard times forced him to sell the younger ones to the Ringling brothers in 1916. He kept his oldest elephants with him at his farm outside Cincinnati. Robinson died in 1921, and one by one, old age claimed three of the four remaining elephants. Petite, nicknamed "Pitt," was the last survivor. Robinson's widow gave her to the Cole Brothers Circus in 1942. Although circus folk claimed Old Pitt was past one hundred, given the longevity of Asian elephants and her performance history, she was indeed elderly and well past her prime, but more realistically her age was around fifty.[20]

The next year, 1943, the circus was traveling across Montana and stopped at Dillon to do a show. The crowd thronged into the exhibition tent to watch the elephants perform. The exhibition ended and the crowd gathered under the Big Top to enjoy the main show. A storm came up suddenly, and a freak bolt of lightning hit the exhibition tent striking Pitt. The elderly elephant died instantly. The electrical jolt stunned the other elephants and circus owner Zach Terrell; they, however, recovered.

Old Pitt had a fine funeral and was buried on the Beaverhead County Fairgrounds. A year later the Cole Brothers Circus again performed at Dillon. Circus folk gathered silently around a granite marker they had paid for. Its careful wording tells Pitt's story and ends with this: "May God Bless Her."[21] A white fence in the middle of barren ground now surrounds the lonely marker. A sapling planted inside the fence, evidence that someone still cares, will hopefully grow to someday shade Old Pitt's final resting place.

ELEVEN

How We Miss Them

In Remembrance

Humans are creative beings and remember those who have passed in individual, sometimes elaborate, novel, or beautifully quiet ways. Funerals, both urban and rural, brought mourners together to pay tribute to the deceased. Sometimes funerals were elaborate and carefully planned, like the tribute to C. M. Russell or the mass funeral for the victims of Butte's warehouse disaster. More often, though, they were small and informal. A cowboy's funeral on the prairie, for example, brought a rare gathering of ranch hands and a reverent pause in work to remember a fallen comrade (see Figure 13). Such a moment, however brief, when people come together, helps the living accept death's finality.

In Montana's most remote areas, the brief period between death and burial sometimes brought neighbors together who played important roles as in the death of Dr. Lon Keith. The work of volunteers at the Keith homestead in 1918 provide a moving testimony to the importance of community. The elderly doctor had come out of his retirement to serve the remote area around Mecaha in Garfield County. He made his final house call traveling fifteen miles in a raging blizzard to set a man's broken leg. By the time he returned to his homestead, the doctor was sick with pneumonia and died three days later. Lilly "Ma" Smith, a practical nurse who had assisted Dr. Keith on dozens of calls, received news of his illness. She packed a bag, hitched up the family sleigh, and rushed to sit with the doctor until the end came. She then cared for his widow, pressed the doctor's best suit, and readied the body for burial. Meanwhile, neighbors arrived with picks and shovels to dig a grave in the frozen, rocky ground nearby. A carpenter set to work fashioning a coffin from the sides of the doctor's work wagon. And finally, Ma Smith removed a dress length of fine gray silk, a cherished Christmas gift from her son, to line the coffin and make a pillow for Dr. Keith's final rest. The sacrifice and generosity of neighbors helped send Dr. Keith on his journey in comfort. Neighbors taking care of each other was, and still is, a way of life.[1]

Funerals, methods of interment, epitaphs, funerary sculpture, memorials, and graveside offerings are some of the ways we care for the dead, celebrate a person's life, and remember them when they are no longer with us. This helps the living move past loss. Open-air interment, earth burial (inhumation), and cremation have been the most common methods of committing loved ones to eternal rest in Montana. Graveside commemorations, however, vary widely and may be lavishly expensive, highly artistic, symbolically complex, or poignantly simple and homemade.

Fear of Burial Alive, Embalming, and Cremation

Before the widespread practice of embalming the dead, the fear of awakening in a coffin, buried alive, was a common terror. There are many grisly descriptions of people who were buried and awakened to panic like this one from Westfield, Massachusetts. The woman had been dead more than a year. Her coffin was being moved to another grave site when those present were curious and opened the lid:

> [They] discovered to their horror, that the corpse was turned over, and the hands of the dead woman were clutched into the hair on her head, while her burial clothing was torn to shreds in many places. There would seem to be little doubt that she was buried alive, and that she met a horrible death in her grave.[2]

The medical profession discounted this and other such reports for the most part; however, in the nineteenth century, numerous devices were patented that provided systems for the dead to communicate should he or she awaken from a coma or trance. Bells placed above the grave, attached to a string in the hand of the deceased, were popular. If the person awakened, he or she could pull the string and ring the bell, alerting the living that the dead was not. The custom may have originated in Germany:

> The greatest danger of premature burial, if there is any at all, is in cases of sudden death in times of epidemic. Over a century ago several mortuary chambers were established in Germany, the first at Weimar, and the second at Munich. Dead bodies were brought to these places and watched closely by medical men. During the first 48 hours after death a bell rope is attached to the hand of the corpse so that in case death was not real the slightest movement would ring the bell. In all of these hundred years only once has the sound of a bell been heard in those mortuary chambers and then it was due to the relaxation of the stiffening hand of the corpse.[3]

A remnant of this practice survives in the MacDonald family cemetery at Fort Connah. There is a bell hung on a wrought iron stake to either side of the grave of Archibald MacDonald. Two more bells flank the entry into a small fenced plot holding the graves of Catherine and Angus MacDonald.

Flowers have been part of funerary rituals for thousands of years, but they did not originally convey the sentiment of today's floral arrangements. Until embalming became the norm, flowers served to cover the odor of decomposition which, depending upon the length of time between death and interment and time of year, could be truly overwhelming. Banks of the most fragrant flowers available covered the casket or coffin if it was closed and if open, filled the viewing area around it.[4] Lilacs were one of the most favored funeral flowers because of their strong scent. Lilac was also the color of mourning. Black clothing could be discarded after a certain period and lavender or lilac-colored garments signaled the transition after deep mourning.

34. Bells in the MacDonald family cemetery at Fort Connah in Lake County assuage age-old fears of being buried alive. Photograph by author.

Until well into the twentieth century, the family parlor typically served as the place for the wake where friends and family paid their last respects. Most historic homes that are at least a century old have seen the dead repose in their parlors. Some believed it was bad luck for a corpse to be carried in or out through the front door. Sometimes homes had two front entries or parlors had exterior doors to facilitate removal of the coffin or casket.

The Civil War brought the practice of embalming the dead to the forefront. Embalming allowed the government to send soldiers' remains home to family for local burial. There were no schools that taught the process until the early twentieth century. Undertakers usually learned embalming by apprenticeship or taught themselves by reading manuals. Embalming was usually done in the deceased's home. The practice, however, was not widespread, especially in rural areas where there was no undertaker and families had to take care of their own. Once embalming schools were established and undertakers began to open funeral homes between 1900 and 1920, the practice became much more commonplace.[5]

When Christianity emerged in Europe, where burning had previously been the typical disposal of the dead, beliefs shifted to the idea that earth burial was the proper care for the deceased. Christians viewed cremation as a pagan practice. But in the nineteenth century, some began to advocate for cremation. Proponents believed the severe overcrowding of cemeteries posed a health threat to the public. They believed that persons who died of cholera, typhoid, diphtheria, smallpox, plague or any number of communicable diseases could still be contagious long after burial. Exposure of bones, they believed, could lead to new epidemics.

Dr. Francis Le Moyne in Washington, Pennsylvania, built the first crematorium in the United States in 1876. Dr. Le Moyne had a patient who was terrified of being buried alive and the doctor was concerned about the health risks of earth burial, so he founded a crematorium. By 1900, many American cemeteries offered this option. In 2016, Montana ranked fifth in the comparative number of cremations in the United States. In 2018, more than 71 percent of all bodies in Montana were cremated.[6] Columbaria on most active cemetery grounds offer permanent storage of ashes.

Mausoleums

Mausoleums are another way Montanans historically commemorated the dead. House-like structures for loved ones who passed on were at first an expression of wealth and social status. Made popular by Queen Victoria after the death of her husband Albert in 1861, these tombs gained in popularity in cemeteries across the United States. Aboveground burials in mausoleums are the norm in Europe and in some places in the United States. In New Orleans, aboveground burials are required to prevent cemeteries from becoming "bone gumbo" during frequent flooding.

Mausoleums add architectural interest to many Montana cemeteries. The Conrad mausoleum, for example, is artfully sited on its prominent point and blends into the wooded landscape at the Conrad Memorial Cemetery. However, some are much more pretentious. The Morony Mausoleum in Hillcrest Cemetery at Deer Lodge boasts an original Tiffany stained glass window. The imposing structure stands alone overlooking Milwaukee Avenue. Built with six crypts to house the family of wealthy First National Bank president John G. Marony in 1916, only he and several others were entombed there. Marony's wife was a Deer Lodge native and built the mausoleum for her husband, herself, and other family members. Marony's mother, who died in 1912, was moved to the mausoleum, but Mrs. Marony did not anticipate her second marriage. She moved out of state and is buried elsewhere. Such changes in family dynamics sometimes profoundly affect burial locations.

The massive sepulcher of wealthy Irish miner Thomas Cruse is Montana's most ostentatious mausoleum, visible from a far distance on Interstate 15. Cruse, his wife, daughter, and several other family members are interred within, and the structure is the focal point of the Catholic Resurrection Cemetery in Helena.

Thomas Cruse was a major benefactor of Helena's Cathedral of St. Helena. Without his funding, the cathedral might not have been built. But the mausoleum is another matter, and its placement is unlike any other in Montana's Catholic cemeteries. A driveway and rows of other graves form a circle around it. The graves of priests and nuns form part of the circle. Smaller mausoleums and large headstones of some of the state's most powerful residents, including wealthy railroad mogul Peter Larson and U.S. senators T. C. Power and Thomas Walsh, form the other half of the circle. These and others all face the Cruse mausoleum. Local rumor has it that as the cemetery was being laid out, Cruse insisted that his mausoleum be central, and may have hinted that funds for the cathedral depended upon that. Additionally, most family crypts have the last name inscribed over the entry, but in this case, it is not merely the name "Cruse" but THOMAS CRUSE cut into the stone.

Although family mausoleums dot Montana cemeteries, above ground mass burials were never common practice. Yet there was a trend after 1900 when better, inexpensive concrete products made crypts housing many families feasible. Progressive-era philosophy encouraged communal activism and the mausoleum movement, offering affordable aboveground interment to ordinary citizens, was one outcome. In 1921, the Consolidated Mausoleum Company advertised communal mausoleums in Montana newspapers. "The present high state of civilization demands," read the ad, "a more humane and sanitary method of taking care of the dead, than found in earth burial."

In 1924, the community of Red Lodge built a multi-family mausoleum along Montana Route 78 in the older portion of the Red Lodge City Cemetery. With more than two hundred burial spaces, it is moisture tight and extremely durable, meant to stand in perpetuity. The massive temple front features heavy bronze doors and enormous Tuscan columns that reinforce the ideas of strength and permanence. True to its purpose, the mausoleum entombs wealthy businessmen and immigrant coal-mining families equally. Communities across the nation bought into this novel idea, and hundreds joined the movement, but the National Register–listed Red Lodge mausoleum is one of only three historic examples identified in Montana.[7] The other two are at Great Falls and Billings.

Mausoleums and aboveground crypts should not be confused with receiving vaults that are often architecturally attractive cemetery features. Such vaults offer temporary storage of remains in winter when the ground is frozen or when interim burial space is needed. The imposing stone storage vault at Helena's Forestvale Cemetery, just inside the historic gateway, was built in the 1890s and is one such example.

In addition to the mausoleums that dot Montana's more formal cemetery grounds, some cemeteries offer chapels and shelters for mourners and visitors. The Dawson County Cemetery at Glendive, for example, dates to the 1880s and includes an iconic, historic chapel, recently refurbished, that has comforted generations of pioneer families. More recently, the Dearborn

Cemetery at Wolf Creek in Lewis and Clark County has a beautiful and sturdy log chapel, built as a memorial to members of the Burggraff family who died in an auto accident in 1956. Shelters are not necessarily religious; sometimes they simply offer respite from inclement weather and benches for rest and reflection. The shelter in the Corvallis Cemetery in Ravalli County is exemplary.

Epitaphs and Embellishments

Epitaphs say something about the deceased or express the grief of the living. Sometimes epitaphs are written by the person before death; sometimes loved ones compose them posthumously. Montana's cemeteries contain hundreds of these, but there is no sadder epitaph that than that of Gussie Bach. Her beautiful headstone at Benton Avenue Cemetery in Helena is of white marble, probably provided by her grief-stricken husband.

Gussie, described as "gentle, courteous, and charitable," died with her newborn daughter after a short illness in 1889. Gussie had previously lost two children, a son who died in 1883 at seven months, and a baby who died in 1884. Buried with her baby daughter in her arms, Gussie's husband Edmund paid her a heart-wrenching, beautiful tribute with this epitaph: "Thus clinging to that slight spar within her arms, the mother drifted out upon the dark and unknown sea."[8]

African American Jack Taylor, buried in Virginia City's Hillside Cemetery, came to Montana in the 1860s. He worked as a teamster and eventually owned horses and cattle. In 1906, he accused Thomas Thexton, a prominent white Madison Valley rancher, of rustling his horses and won the lawsuit. Thexton was sentenced to a year at the state penitentiary.[9] Taylor was a well-known character. His headstone, rather plain but substantial, has an epitaph that speaks to the man and his work ethic: "As long as the earth remaineth, seed time and harvest shall not cease."

Between 1875 and 1890, Benton Avenue was Helena's nonsectarian burial ground. As the old cemetery was being relocated from the Central School site to Benton in 1875, Wilbur Sanders, then president of the Montana Historical Society, retrieved the wooden headboard of Langford Peel, a desperado killed in a bar fight in 1867. He placed it in the attic of his Ewing Street home. Peel was reburied in an unmarked grave at Benton Avenue and the headboard lay in Sanders's attic until 1928. New homeowners found it and gave it to the Montana Historical Society.[10] The tombstone, preserved in the society's museum collection, is five feet tall and expertly carved. The enigmatic inscription reads in part, "Vengence [sic] is mine, sayeth the lord. I know that my redeemer liveth." Peel's contemporaries viewed it not as religious, but rather as a curse against Peel's murderer.

Montana's most famous epitaph is that of Frank Little who is buried in Butte's Mountain View Cemetery. His grave is one of the most visited.[11] On the heels of the Granite Mountain-Speculator Mine disaster and during a time of labor unrest in July 1917, the union and anti-war activist arrived in Butte. On the executive board of the Industrial Workers of the World, Little was there to organize miners. He was kidnapped from his boarding house on August 1, 1917, brutally murdered and his body hung on a railroad trestle. A mile-long procession followed Little to his burial in an unmarked grave. Years later a Butte businessman— ironically himself a capitalist—commissioned a headstone. The epitaph reads: "Slain by Capitalist Interests for Organizing and Inspiring His Fellow Men."

Headstones in many Montana cemeteries display the emblems of organizations. The Masons' square and compass; the star of the Order of the Eastern Star; and the three interlinked circles—symbolizing friendship, love, and truth—of the Independent Order of Oddfellows are all prevalent in Montana's cemeteries. Emblems of the Woodmen of the World, Knights of Pythias, the Benevolent Protective Order of Elks, the Fraternal Order of Eagles, and others also commonly appear on headstones, leaving clues for the visitor about the deceased's activities.

Among the most common tombstone symbols are hands and fingers. These are expressive parts of the human body and thus figure prominently in tombstone art. A finger pointing up refers to the ascent to heaven and the afterlife while a finger pointing

35. One of Montana's most visited grave sites is that of Frank Little in Butte's Mountain View Cemetery. Photograph by Jon Axline.

down usually symbolizes the hand of God. Clasped hands, representing a final farewell, can refer to friendship, as in fraternal organizations, or the final goodbye between a child and a parent. If the cuffs at the wrists are male and female, it may mean the bond of holy matrimony.

Urns and drapery are also common features found on tombstones. The connection between urns and death goes back many centuries to the early Greeks and Romans. Cremation was a common practice during the classical period and urns were the receptacles of ashes. Urns could be in various shapes, even square. Regardless of shape, such receptacles were always called "urns." The word comes from the Latin *uro*, meaning "burn." Urns are often associated with drapery. A death in the family required

How We Miss Them

that mirrors either be turned to the wall or covered with draping until the funeral was over. Sometimes this was a religious custom. Some believed that this act kept evil spirits, only visible through mirrors, away from the house. Others believed it necessary to avoid the vanity of seeing one's own image during times of deep mourning. Some believed that the first person to see his or her reflection after a death would be the next to die. Black crepe was commonly used for draping.

Although the children of territorial legislator Oscar Sedman of Madison County recovered from measles, an often-fatal childhood disease, their father was not so lucky. He died in Helena during the legislative session in 1881, the first legislator to die during a session. The doorknob to the house of representatives and Sedman's desk were draped in black crepe and his empty chair turned to the wall.[12] The practice translates to tombstone art. Cloth draped over urns and across headstones symbolizes the veil between life and death.

If a person had no portrait at the time of his or her death, it was common to take a post mortem photograph lest the family forget what the person looked like. Portraits affixed to monuments also served as a symbolic replacement for the individual and assured that loved ones would remember. The first attempts at fixing portraits on headstones were daguerreotypes, ambrotypes, or tintypes placed in a niche carved into the stone and then covered with glass.[13] The Nevada City Cemetery has a surviving example in the crudely made tombstone of five-year-old Auguste and four-year-old Lillie Hermsmeyer, brother and sister, who died days apart in December 1876. The portrait, although unrecognizable, remains under heavy beveled glass affixed to their shared headstone.

Better preserved are later examples of porcelain portraits. The process of burning a photograph onto porcelain was developed in Germany and American companies also patented this technique. Carbon County's Bearcreek Cemetery has an unusual grouping of headstones that display the Cyrillic lettering of Eastern European immigrants. Many of these headstones include beautifully preserved porcelain portraits of the deceased.

36. Coal miners and their families buried at Bearcreek Cemetery reflect Slavic origins with tombstones inscribed in Cyrillic; many include portraits of the deceased. Photograph by Jon Axline.

Montana has beautiful examples of marble statuary art depicting angels and contemplative figures. One of the most spectacular is that at the grave site of twenty-year-old Katherine Sligh at Forestvale Cemetery in Helena. Her father, Philipsburg physician Dr. James Sligh, was unable to prevent her death from rheumatic heart disease in 1896. Her illness was sudden and her death swift, a month before her marriage to Thomas Marlow, wealthy president of the Montana National Bank.[14] Marlow was grief-stricken and provided her burial plot in Forestvale Cemetery; he did not marry for nearly a decade after her death. Marlow probably paid for the stunning, unsigned Carrera marble sculpture that crowns her monument. The delicate figure holds a wreath of mourning in one hand while the other rests lightly on her cheek. The epitaph reads:

> There is no death. What seems so is transition.
> This life of mortal breath
> Is but a suburb of the life Elysian
> Whose portal we call death.

Hundreds of young children are memorialized in various ways in Montana's cemeteries. Grave sites of babies are sometimes fashioned into bassinets with different types of delicate fencing, symbolically providing the child with eternal sleep. Lambs for innocence and child angels typically ornament children's tombstones. Shoes and socks are also a common thematic ornament, symbolizing unrealized potential; one shoe is generally upright and the other poignantly on its side.

Although other artists also carved similar examples, at least one of Alonzo K. Prescott's carvers specialized in children's tombstones in the shape of a child's tufted chair. Clothing drapes across the back, a hat is cast aside, and a small pair of shoes lies tucked underneath folds of drapery. A signed example, that of siblings Clarita and Charley Warren who died in 1880 and 1886, is at Butte's Mount Moriah Cemetery. Three more, two of them signed, lie in the same area at Helena's Benton Avenue Cemetery. One marks the grave of Jane Stanchfield who died at six months in 1886. Another is that of two-year-old Pauline Dunn,

37. Refurbished wooden crosses in the Mayn Cemetery at White Sulphur Springs commemorate a brother and sister who died of the Spanish influenza. Photograph by author.

and a third that of siblings Felix Warren and Norma Alada Kuehn, ages one and four. Pauline and the Kuehn children died of diphtheria during a devastating epidemic in 1885. The epitaph on the Kuehn children's stone reads: "How we miss them." Another signed example is at Hillcrest Cemetery in Deer Lodge, marking the resting place of three-year-old Katie Blessinger who also died of diphtheria during an epidemic in 1888. A final example at Sunset Hills in Bozeman marks the grave of Jamie D. Yerkes who was five when he died of pneumonia in 1890. These numerous examples end in 1890, perhaps signaling the end of the anonymous artist's Montana career.

Montanans have always found unique ways to memorialize their loved ones. Mayn Cemetery at White Sulphur Springs in Meagher County includes several highly personalized and poignant tombstones. A Ringling family tombstone with a horse and an elephant recalls the family's circus fame and a horse and rider with the epitaph, "He's home now," memorializes a horseman. Jimmy Duane Schrader's 2001 substantial granite tombstone reflects his fascination with trains, but another clue to his worldly interests is a sculptured, painted puppy that sits waiting on the corner of the granite base.

Many grave sites across the state recall the Spanish influenza pandemic that swept the nation in 1918–19, and wooden crosses are commonplace throughout Montana's cemeteries. However, at Mayn Cemetery, Herbert Schwab made two wooden crosses for the graves of his son and daughter who died of the flu within two weeks of each other in 1919. Schwab family descendants refurbished the two free-standing crosses in 2007.

Symbolic Tree Trunks and Enclosures

Tree trunks and branches are a common symbol in Montana's historic cemeteries. Italian stonecutters Michael Jacobs and Pasqual Petosa took that symbolism to the highest level. They arrived at Columbus, Montana, in 1900 to work at the Montana Sandstone Company. For the next several decades, the two produced stunning carved sandstone tombstones for the National Register–listed Mountain View Cemetery at Columbus in Stillwater County. Although neither artist signed his work, gravestone carving was their specialty and they were master craftsmen. One large obelisk, exhibited at the St. Louis World's Fair in 1904, became the cemetery's focal point. Marking the Wimsett family plot, it is twelve feet in height and the largest of some thirty-one other sandstone sculptures that depict tree-stumps or log themes. No two are alike and locals attribute most of them to Jacobs and Petrosa.[15]

Michael Jacobs died in 1927 and Pasqual Petosa in 1939. With the deaths of these talented craftsman, the rich folk traditions they wove into their work could not be duplicated and died with them.

The Columbus headstones include rich and complicated symbolism. Tree-stump tombstones may be originally linked to the fraternal Woodmen of the World (W.O.W.), but they are not limited to members of that fraternal group. Many of Montana's cemeteries have examples of the genre although they are not of sandstone. The tree trunk symbolizes life cut short. Cut off or bro-

38. The Wimsett family monument, exhibited at the 1904 St. Louis World's Fair, is a focal point among the artistic tree trunk tombstones of Michael Jacobs and Pasqual Petosa in the Mountain View Cemetery at Columbus. Photograph by author.

ken branches may indicate the death of a family member. Intertwined logs represent the love of a husband and wife. Rings in the end of the stump can indicate the age of the deceased while cracks interrupting the rings may indicate children born in the marriage. Other symbols worked into the overall designs carry traditional meanings. A dove symbolizes peace; a morning glory refers to the resurrection and bonds of love; a fern symbolizes goals unfinished; ivy stands for fidelity and immortality. An anchor symbolizes steadfastness and hope. If its chain is broken, it signifies the end of life. Anchors also can denote the deceased was a mariner or seaman, but they do not always have that connotation. Anchors frequently appear in the Columbus monuments.

Fences of wood and wrought iron surround many family plots across the state. While wood enclosures are frequently in a state of decay, wrought iron fencing is remarkably durable. Iron fencing is somehow comforting and reminiscent of the sturdy pioneers who wished to assure their loved one of perpetual remembrance. Wrought iron fencing sometimes displays beautiful ornamental elements. One unusual example surrounds the Benton Avenue plot of Agnes Merrill, whose name and the date—1878—remain beautifully painted on the entry gate. Pineapples, a common symbol of welcome and hospitality, form the four corners of the fence. The unusual advertisement is a perfect expression well-fitted to the deceased. Agnes was a prostitute who evidently welcomes visitors as hospitably in death as she did in life.

Lacy, delicate wrought iron fencing surrounds the graves of two young daughters of Butte's copper king William A. Clark in Hillcrest Cemetery at Deer Lodge. The Clark family settled at Deer Lodge long before Butte copper made Clark wealthy. The imported tombstone commemorates both children, an infant who died in 1874 and the other, two-year-old Jessie, who died in 1878. The stone is signed, "J.W. Bray, Fecit, N.Y." Jessie's funeral was widely attended and the *New North-west* noted, "Lying in a casket of satin, her head turned aside as though sleeping, the expression natural as life and choicest flowers disposed around, it seemed almost impossible to realize that the little one was dead."[16] Such was the uncertainty of childhood in the nineteenth century.

39. Lacy wrought iron fencing encloses the plot of copper king
W. A. Clark's two small daughters at Hillcrest Cemetery in Deer Lodge.
Photograph by author.

Montana's White Crosses

Since 1953, American Legion posts across Montana have marked
the sites of traffic fatalities with white crosses. They are intended
to remind motorists to drive carefully. The idea took root in Missoula County after six local people lost their lives in traffic accidents during the Labor Day weekend in 1952. Floyd Eaheart of
Hellgate Post No. 27 conceived the idea. The Montana legislature approved the program and every Montana governor since
has endorsed it. Not all fatality sites receive markers. Sometimes
families request no marker, and sometimes crosses are removed
when roadways are reconstructed.

The Fatality Marker Safety Program (previously called the
White Cross Program) has placed more than two thousand white
metal crosses along Montana's highways and roads, enough to
fill a five-acre cemetery. Visitors sometimes find the stark white
crosses unnerving as they travel the state. That is their purpose.

How We Miss Them

The crosses are not designed as memorials, and decorations are discouraged. However, many interpret them that way and families add flowers, wreaths, mementos, stuffed animals, and seasonal decorations. The crosses not only assuage the grief of those left behind, but also remind passing motorists that life is fleeting and can end in an instant.

40. White crosses along Montana's roadways are sometimes personalized with flowers or mementos. The addition of a canine silhouette memorializes a beloved pet that died with his owners. Photograph by author.

Afterword

In the past decade, cemetery preservation has received some attention in Montana through the efforts of the Montana Historical Society and the Montana History Foundation. While this is a topic beyond the scope of the present work, preservation of our cemeteries is important in facilitating the interpretation of local community and state history. The Montana Historical Society has offered numerous public workshops with hands-on demonstrations in the proper materials and techniques used in preserving and repairing tombstones. The Montana History Foundation has funded historic research and cemetery preservation projects across the state, and in 2018 with a grant from the National Center for Preservation Technology and Training, a unit of the National Park Service, a three-day workshop included training in various aspects of the latest technology. Presentations and resources are available at www.mthistory.org.

Notes

1. Death, Burial among First Montanans

1. Larry Lahren, "Anzick Researchers Snub State and Native Tribes," *Montana Pioneer* (April 2014) at https://montanapioneer.com/anzick-researchers -snub-state-native-tribes/.

2. Douglas H. MacDonald, *Montana before History: 11,000 Years of Hunter Gatherers in the Rockies and Plains* (Missoula MT: Mountain Press, 2012), 35–36; Doug Peacock, "Voices of Bones," *Outside* (February 2000): 66.

3. Morten Rasmussen et al., "The Genome of a Late Pleistocene human from a Clovis burial site in western Montana," *Nature* 506, no. 7487 (2014): 225–29; Brett French, "Remains of Ancient Child Ceremoniously Reburied," Billings *Gazette,* June 28, 2014.

4. J. Scott Jones, "The Anzick Site: Analysis of a Clovis Burial Assemblage" (PhD diss., Oregon State University, 1996), 181, 186–87, https://ir.library .oregonstate.edu/concern/graduate_thesis_or_dissertations/mw22v9109; Samuel Stockton White V, "The Anzick Artifacts: A High-Technology Forager Tool Assemblage" (PhD diss., University of Montana, 2019), 147–54, https:// scholarworks.umt.edu/etd/11338.

5. George W. Gill and Gerald R. Clark, "Late Plains Archaic Burial from Iron Jaw Creek, Southwestern Montana," *Plains Anthropologist* 28, no. 101 (1983): 191–98.

6. Leslie B. Davis et. al., "An Avonlea Inhumation at Split-Rock Ridge, Big Dry Creek Valley, Eastern Montana High Plains," *Plains Anthropologist* 62, no. 241 (2017): 32–66.

7. Davis et al., "Avonlea Inhumation," 55–54, 62.

8. James F. Brooks, "Sing Away the Buffalo: Faction and Fission on the Northern Plains," in *Beyond Subsistence: Plains Archaeology and Post Processual Critique,* ed. Philip Duke and Michael C. Wilson (Tuscaloosa: University of Alabama Press, 1995), 150–54.

9. William Mulloy, "The Hagen Site: A Prehistoric Village on the Lower

Yellowstone," *Montana Publications in the Social Sciences,* Reprints in Anthropology, vol. 4, no. 1 (Missoula: University of Montana, 1942): 9–10.

10. Jeffrey W. Kinney, "Hagen Site, 24DW1: A Review of Historical Data and a Reassessment of Its Ceramic Assemblage and Position in Northern Plains Prehistory," (master's thesis, University of Montana, 1996): 10. https:// scholarworks.umt.edu/cgi/viewcontent.cgi?article=3522&context=etd; MacDonald, *Montana before History,* 136.

11. W. H. Banfill, "Prehistoric Indian Art," *Montana News Association Inserts,* December 2, 1927.

12. MacDonald, *Montana before History,* 53, 76.

13. Glendolin Damon Wagner, "Indian Cave on Coburn Hill Near Billings Was Home to Semi-Civilized Tribe 1,000 Years Ago," *Fergus County Argus* (Lewistown MT), February 28, 1938.

14. Wagner, "Indian Cave."

15. Larry Lahren, *Homeland: An Archaeologist's View of Yellowstone Country's Past* (Livingstone MT: Cayuse Press, 2006), 100.

16. French, "Remains of Ancient Child Ceremoniously Reburied."

2. Customs of the Upper Missouri Tribes

1. Edwin Thompson Denig, *Indian Tribes of the Upper Missouri,* ed. J. N. B. Hewitt. Forty-sixth Annual Report of the Bureau of American Ethnology to the Secretary of the Smithsonian Institution, 1928–1929 (Washington DC: Government Printing Office, 1930), 571–76, https://www.gutenberg.org/files /49557/49557-h/49557-h.htm.

2. Denig, *Indian Tribes of the Upper Missouri,* 576.

3. John C. Ewers, *The Blackfeet: Raiders on the Northwestern Plains* (Norman: University of Oklahoma, 1958), 106–7.

4. C. M. Russell, "The Ghost Horse," *Trails Plowed Under* (New York: Doubleday, 1927), Project Gutenberg of Australia ebooks 2007 at http://gutenberg.net .au/ebooks07/0700941h.html#ch2-10; Ellen Baumler, *More Montana Moments* (Helena: Montana Historical Society Press, 2012), 70–72.

5. Denig, *Indian Tribes of the Upper Missouri,* 573.

6. H. C. Yarrow, *Introduction to the Study of Mortuary Customs among the North American Indians* (Washington DC: Government Printing Office, 1880), 103, Project Gutenberg, https://www.gutenberg.org/files/11398/11398-h/11398 -h.htm#page103.

7. Yarrow, *Introduction to the Study of Mortuary Customs,* 161.

8. Lieutenant James H. Bradley, *The March of the Montana Column: A Prelude to the Custer Disaster,* ed. Edgar I. Stewart (1961; repr. Norman: University of Oklahoma Press, 1991), 112–13; Fanny Kelly, *Narrative of My Captivity Among the Sioux Indians* (Hartford CT: Mutual Publishing Company, 1873).

9. P. W. Norris, quoted in Yarrow, *Introduction to the Study of Mortuary Customs,* 153.

10. James Beckwourth, chapter 18 in *Life and Adventures of James P. Beck-wourth*, (New York: Harper & Bros, 1856), 260, accessed May 3, 2020, https://user.xmission.com/~drudy/mtman/html/beckwourth/#ch18.

11. Beckwourth, *Life and Adventures of James P. Beckwourth*, 260.

12. Denig, *Indian Tribes of the Upper Missouri*, 574; Ewers, *The Blackfeet*, 107.

13. Lawrence B. Palladino, *Indian and White in the Northwest; A History of Catholicity in Montana, 1831–1891*, rev. ed. (Lancaster PA: Wickersham Publishing, 1922), 81.

3. Tragedy beyond Description

1. David Thompson, *David Thompson's Narrative of his Explorations in Western America 1784–1812*, ed. J. B. Terrell, Greenwood facsimile edition (Toronto: Champlain Society, 1916), 336–37, accessed May 3, 2020. https://archive.org/stream/davidthompsonsna00thom#page/110/mode/2up.

2. Hudson's Bay Company pilot Mitchell Oman related this to Thompson, 322–23; Volney Steele, M. D., *Bleed Blister and Purge* (Missoula MT: Mountain Press, 2005), 37.

3. E. Wagner Stearn and Allen E. Stearn, *The Effect of Smallpox on the Destiny of the Amerindian* (Boston: Bruce Humphries, 1945), 93.

4. Charles Larpenteur, Chapter 7 in *Forty Years a Trader on the Missouri River*, (Chicago: Lakeside Press, 1933), 37–38, accessed May 3, 2020, http://www.manuellisaparty.com/articles/pfd's/larpenteur.pdf.

5. Michael Stephen Kennedy, ed., *The Assiniboines: From the Accounts of the Old Ones Told to First Boy* (Norman: University of Oklahoma Press, 1961), 168–69.

6. Bradley, *The March of the Montana Column*, 224–25.

7. Donna Healy, "Smallpox Fears Stir Memories of Heavy Toll Indians Suffered," *Billings Gazette*, January 25, 2003.

8. Steele, *Bleed Blister and Purge*, 260.

9. Diane J. Pearson, "Lewis Cass and the Politics of Disease: The Indian Vaccination Act of 1832." *Wicazo Sa Review* 18, no. 2(2003): 9–35, doi:10.1353/wic.2003.0017.

10. Bradley, *The March of the Montana Column*, 226–27.

11. Michael P. Malone, Richard B. Roeder, and William Lang, *Montana: A History of Two Centuries*, rev ed. (Seattle: University of Washington, 1991), 59.

12. Edwin Thompson Denig, *Five Indian Tribes of the Upper Missouri*, ed. John C. Ewers (Norman: University of Oklahoma, 1961), 71–72; Ewers, *The Blackfeet*, 106–7.

13. Dan Sleeping Bear, "Indian Smallpox Story," *Montana News Association Inserts*, December 30, 1934.

14. "Cost of the Smallpox," *Anaconda Standard*, November 23, 1893; "Mortality of the Year," *Anaconda Standard*, January 8, 1894.

15. "Official Bulletin," *Anaconda Standard*, July 15, 1893, and "Gophers at

Work," *Anaconda Standard*, September 27, 1893; Vera Haffey, "Smelter City Cemeteries," *Montana Standard*, October 29, 2000.

16. Donna Healy, "Smallpox Outbreak Traced to Costumes Shipped in for Ball," *Billings Gazette*, January 26, 2003; "Will No Longer Quarantine for Smallpox," *Big Timber Pioneer*, July 15, 1909; "Smallpox Patients Merely Placarded," *Great Falls Tribune*, May 29, 1919. Ellen Leahy, "Montana Fever: Smallpox and the Montana State Board of Health," *Montana The Magazine of Western History* 53:2 (Summer 2003), 32–45.

17. Dr. Eddy Crowley, personal communication with the author, December 22, 2017.

18. Tracy Thornton, "No Laughing Matter," *Butte Montana Standard*, July 21, 1996; University of Montana, "The Influenza Pandemic," Memorial Row, accessed August 10, 2020, https://www.umt.edu/memorialrow/influenza/default.php.

4. Before There Was Billings

1. Joe Medicine Crow insisted on this wording for the Indian Highway Marker installed at Boot Hill Cemetery. Personal communication with the author on several occasions in 1993.

2. Joe Medicine Crow's story, retold in a letter from Stuart Conner to Dr. Ann Johnson, May 6, 1981, in possession of the author; Henry Old Coyote, quoted in Roger Clawson, "Old Coyote a Wise Man in 2 Worlds," *Billings Gazette*, May 6, 1988.

3. Roger Clawson, "Legend of Sacrifice Cliff Said White Man's Tale," *Billings Gazette*, December 2, 1970; Clair Johnson, "The Legend and the Rock," *Billings Gazette*, December 20, 2014. So-called Sacrifice Cliff is on the opposite side of the Yellowstone River south of I-90, not where the leap supposedly occurred.

4. Bradley, *The March of the Montana Column*, 52–54.

5. Mary Pickett, "'Face-on-the-Rims' Origins Unknown to Historians," *Billings Gazette*, August 19, 2006.

6. Glendolin Damon Wagner and Dr. William A. Allen, *Blankets and Moccasins: Plenty Coups and his People, the Crows* (Caldwell ID: Caxton Printers, 1936), 203–4. Stu Connor, personal files in possession of the author, does not believe that these burials were all the result of one wave of smallpox.

7. Dale L. Hutchinson and Jeffrey M. Mitchem, "Correlates of Contact: Epidemic Diseases in Archaeological Contexts," *Historical Archaeology* 35:2 (June 2001): 61.

8. Connor, files in possession of the author.

9. Ewers, *The Blackfeet*, 53–54; Hiram Martin Chittenden, *The American Fur Trade of the Far West* (New York: Harper, 1902), 3:154–55, accessed May 3, 2020, https://archive.org/stream/americanfurtrade01chit#page/152/mode/2up/search/Immel.

10. Katy Hestand, Yellowstone County Places, "Indian Rock—Billings Montana," MTGenWeb Project, http://www.mtgenweb.com/yellowstone/places/indian_rock.htm.

11. Harold Rixon quote transcribed in the Stuart Connor files, dated October 1, 1960, in possession of the author.

12. Mary Pickett, "Secrets of the Rims," *Billings Gazette*, August 20, 2006.

5. Conflict, Misfortune, Transitions

1. Frederick Allen, *A Decent and Orderly Lynching: The Montana Vigilantes* (Norman: University of Oklahoma, 2004), 134.

2. Michael Leeson, *History of Montana 1739–1885* (Chicago: Warner, Beers, 1885), 271, tells this story implicating the infamous sheriff of Bannack, Henry Plummer.

3. Thomas Dimsdale, *The Vigilantes of Montana*, Western Frontier Library (Norman: University of Oklahoma, 1953), 1:124. Dimsdale also implicates Plummer.

4. Nathaniel Langford, *Vigilante Days and Ways*, ed. Richard B. Roeder (Helena: American and World Geographic Publishing, 1996), 197–204, is the most detailed account. See also Ellen Baumler, *Ghosts of the Last Best Place* (Charleston SC: The History Press, 2016), 17–21.

5. Susan Badger Doyle, ed. *Journeys to the Land of Gold: Emigrant Diaries from the Bozeman Trail, 1863–1866* (Helena: Montana Historical Society Press, 2002), 2:542–43; Thomas diary, SC 1303, Montana Historical Society Archives, Helena, Montana.

6. Dave Walter, "The Thomas Tragedy on the Yellowstone," *Montana Campfire Tales* (Helena: Falcon Press, 1997), 19–31; Baumler, *Montana Moments*, 79–80.

7. Rodney G. Thomas, "Indian Casualties of the Little Big Horn Battle," in *Rubbing out Long Hair (Pehin Hanska Kasota): The American Indian Story of the Little Big Horn in Art and Word* (Spanaway WA: Elk Press, 2009), accessed May 3, 2020, http://www.littlebighorn.info/Articles/IndianCasualties.pdf.

8. Bradley, *The March of the Montana Column*, 172.

9. Bob Reece, "Interment of the Custer Dead," Friends of the Little Bighorn Battlefield, accessed May 3, 2020, http://www.friendslittlebighorn.com/dusttodust.htm.

10. Lieutenant James Bradley letter to the editor, *Helena Weekly Herald*, July 27, 1876, p. 7.

11. "Nuggets of News," *New North-west*, June 27, 1890.

12. Malone, Roeder, and Lang, *Montana*, 134–39, offers a concise discussion of the battle and the Nez Perce retreat.

13. John B. Catlin reminiscence, SC 520, Montana Historical Society Research Center Archives, Helena, Montana.

14. Douglas D. Scott, "A Sharp Little Affair: The Archaeology of the Big Hole Battlefield," *Reprints in Anthropology* 45 (1994); revised for PDF pub-

lication (June 2009): 46–47, accessed May 3, 2020, https://irma.nps.gov /Datastore/DownloadFile/441695.

15. Paul C. Phillips, *Medicine in the Making of Montana* (Missoula: Montana State University Press, 1962), 88; Palladino, *Indian and White in the Northwest*, 413.

16. G. O. Shields, *The Battle of the Big Hole* (Chicago: Rand McNally, 1889), 80–81, accessed May 3, 2020, https://babel.hathitrust.org/cgi/pt?id=wu .89073054322;view=1up;seq=13.

17. Andrew Garcia, *Tough Trip through Paradise 1878–1879*, ed. Bennett H. Stein (Moscow: University of Idaho, 2001), 309–10.

18. Shields, *Battle of the Big Hole*, 101–3.

19. "Romance of Two Rings," *Anaconda Standard*, February 23, 1900.

20. There are numerous versions of the murder of Hugh Boyle and the Head Chief-Young Mule story. The most reliable are those of Carol Bailey, posted on the Miles City.com History and Genealogy Forum, accessed May 3, 2020, http://milescity.com/forums/posts/view/328613#328660. Also in Margot Liberty and John Stands-In-Timber, *Cheyenne Memories* (New Haven CT: Yale University, 1967); Baumler, *Ghosts of the Last Best Place*, 30–36.

21. "Murderous Cheyennes," *Daily Yellowstone Journal* September 11, 1890; "They Died Game," *Yellowstone Journal*, September 17, 1890; "Victim a Lad," *Helena Independent Record*, September 13, 1890; "Willing to be Shot," *Helena Daily Independent*, January 24, 1891.

6. Death in Early Communities

1. For example, an inventory taken of all cemeteries in Helena in 1883 revealed that only one quarter of the graves in the city were marked. "Our Cemeteries," *Helena Daily Herald*, June 1, 1883.

2. Joel Overholser, *Fort Benton: World's Innermost Port* (Fort Benton MT: River and Plains Society, 2000), 19.

3. Overholser, *Fort Benton*, 115.

4. Riverside Cemetery, Chouteau County records at findagrave.com.

5. Lucylle H. Evans, *St. Mary's in the Rocky Mountains*, rev. ed. (Stevensville: Montana Creative Consultants, 1976), 86–87.

6. Palladino, *Indian and White in the Northwest*, 58–59.

7. David Murray, "Cemetery Brings to Life 150 Years of History at Fort Shaw," *Great Falls Tribune*, July 6, 2017; "Death Takes Two from the Home," *Great Falls Tribune*, November 23, 1908; "Death Claims a Third Child," *Great Falls Tribune*, November 29, 1908.

8. "Veterans of Three Wars Buried in National Cemetery," *Helena Independent Record*, September 5, 1948.

9. Robert E. Miller, *Hands of the Workmen* (Helena: State Publishing, 1966), 6–8. According to Montana's Masonic lore, in the vigilante warning, 3–7–77, the 77 refers to the number of Masons who attended the Bell funeral.

10. Project Archeology of the Extreme History Project has noted many unmarked graves outside the fenced cemetery proper.

11. Lew Callaway, "Thoroughbred," Big Sandy, *Mountaineer*, May 22, 1930.

12. "Local Items," *Montana Post*, Oct 7, 1865.

13. Phillips, *Medicine in the Making of Montana*, 57. Oddly, Phillips writes that an epidemic of typhoid raged in Virginia City in 1863–1864 but no one died. Perhaps "mountain fever," a non-specific malady that also plagued mining camps, was actually the cause of the Daltons' deaths.

14. Grace Stone Coates, "Mrs. Mathilda Thibadeau Crossed the Plains with the first Fisk Expedition," *Great Falls Tribune*, February 7, 1932: Edwin Ruthven Purple, *Perilous Passage: A Narrative of the Montana Gold Rush 1862–1863*, ed. Kenneth N. Owens (Helena: Montana Historical Society Press, 1995), 142n95, 143.

15. Calloway, "Thoroughbred."

16. Ah Tong's funeral is discussed in chapter 9; for Martin Lyon's murder, see Ellen Baumler, "The Body in the Bathtub," *Spirit Tailings* (Helena: Montana Historical Society Press, 2002), 15–19.

17. Phil Connelly, "George Lane and his Famous Foot," *Hamilton Ravalli Republic*, November 17, 2017.

18. "An Old Acquaintance Drowned," White Cloud, Kansas, *Kansas Chief*, July 26, 1866.

19. Charleen Spalding, *Benton Avenue Cemetery: A Pioneer Resting Place* (Helena: Pioneer Tales Publishing, 2010), 299–306.

20. "Dug up a Skeleton," *Helena Daily Independent*, April 23, 1900; "Bones Thought to Be Daniels," *Independent-Ledger* (Thompson Falls, Sanders County), September 30, 1931.

21. See chapter 7 for further discussion of this site.

22. Susan Olp, "Boothill Cemetery Holds onto Tales of Area's Early Days," *Billings Gazette*, October 24, 2014.

23. Ellen Baumler, "Historical Reflections," *Montana The Magazine of Western History* 50:4 (Winter 2000) 74–75; Baumler, *Montana Moments*, 118–19.

24. "Two Boys Killed," *Helena Independent*, September 29, 1889; "A Mysterious Affair," *Butte Daily Miner*, October 1, 1889.

25. "Murder and Suicide: A Double Tragedy on the Benton Road," *Helena Weekly Herald*, March 4, 1886; "The Moore Tragedy: A Doubtful Verdict," *Helena Independent-Record*, March 2, 1886.

7. Dead and Buried Twice

1. Vera Haffey, "Superfund to Benefit Anaconda Cemetery," *Montana Standard*, June 21, 2005.

2. "Corps Plans Relocation of Graves at Libby Dam," *Missoulian*, June 26, 1969.

3. Mary Ellen Stubb, Missoula Cemetery Sexton, "Missoula Burial Sites," unpublished manuscript, n.d., copy in possession of author.

4. Audra Browman Papers, MSS 468, Series I, Box 1, f36, Mansfield Library Archives and Special Collections, University of Montana, Missoula; Allan Mathews, "Lower Rattlesnake Historic District," National Register of Historic Places nomination, 1998, Montana State Historic Preservation Office, Helena, Montana.

5. See for example "Gone to Confucius," *Missoulian* May 22, 1893; "Poor Hong Kee," *Weekly Missoulian*, August 15, 1894.

6. "Grave of Chinese Found in Street; Bones Are Missing," *Missoulian*, October 22, 1937.

7. "Most of Skeleton is Uncovered," *Missoulian*, October 29, 1974.

8. Katie Baumler, "Mystery on Cherry Street" (senior project Power Point presentation, Anthropology Department, University of Montana, 2008); "Died," *Helena Weekly Herald*, May 16, 1872.

9. Sallie Davenport Davidson, SC606, Montana Historical Society Research Center Archives; *Montana News Inserts*, Mrs. M. E. Plassman, "Mrs. W. H. Parkinson, Pioneer of 1864, Crossed Plains Comfortably in Carriage," August 11, 1928.

10. "Grave Marker Given to State," *Philipsburg Mail*, January 13, 1928; undated letter from Lucille Topping to Lucy Baker, SC 1012 f1/7, Montana Historical Society Research Center Archives, Helena, Montana.

11. Dick Roesgen, "Cemetery May Lie in Highway's Path," *Helena Independent Record*, August 31, 1983; Ann Joyce, "Old Bones from One Body," *Helena Independent Record*, September 2, 1983; Michael Crater, "School Grave Dates to Turn of Century," *Helena Independent Record*, September 17, 1983; Letter from Charline Smith, University of Montana, to Mickey Nelson, Office of the Lewis and Clark County Coroner, September 15, 1983, copy in possession of author.

12. Carolyn Bright, "Construction Crew Inadvertently Unearths Graves," *Helena Independent Record*, November 11, 2004; Jesse Chaney, "Excavators Unearth Human Remains under Helena Road," *Helena Independent Record*, May 30, 2018. The disposition of the contents of the Robinson Park burials is unclear. Some of the bones may rest with the county coroner, some at the University of Montana, and some may have been reburied in the county cemetery or other cemeteries.

13. Tom Donovan, *Hanging Around the Big Sky, Book One* (Great Falls MT: Portage Meadow Publishing, 2007), 605, 607. Radersburg, now in Broadwater County, was originally the seat of Jefferson County. Until 1983, Montana law required all legal hangings to be conducted in the county where the crime was committed.

14. See Ellen Baumler, *Montana Chillers* (Helena: Farcountry Press, 2009), 112–21.

15. "Dead Sleep in Peace," *Dillon Tribune*, December 6, 1907.

16. "The Lewis-Clark Tragedy," *New North-west*, August 24, 1883; "Lewis

Murder Case," *Helena Weekly Herald*, October 25, 1883; "Town Talk," *Billings Herald*, October 27, 1883.

17. Reverend Kyle Johnston, "A Love Beyond the Grave," *Dillon Tribune*, October 17, 2001; Baumler, *More Montana Moments*, 33–34.

18. "Commissioners Proceedings," *Big Timber Pioneer*, August 10, 1933; Baumler, *Montana Moments*, 84.

19. Mike Stark, "Rags-to-Riches Miner to be Reburied in Funeral Celebration," *Billings Gazette*, August 26, 2005; Marge Cargo in Voice of the Reader, "Cemetery Wasn't the End for Pioneer Pete Zortman," *Billings Gazette*, September 2, 2005.

8. Evolution of Beautiful Grounds

1. "Père Lachaise Cemetery: A Brief History." Accessed May 4, 2020. http://northstargallery.com/pages/perehist.htm.

2. David Charles Sloane, *The Last Great Necessity* (Baltimore: Johns Hopkins University Press, 1991), 3.

3. Keith Eggener interview with Rebecca Greenfield, "Our First Public Parks: The Forgotten History of Cemeteries," *Atlantic*, March 16, 2011, http://www.theatlantic.com/national/archive/2011/03/our-first-public-parks-the -forgotten-history-of-cemeteries/71818/.

4. Richard E. Meyer, ed. *Cemeteries and Gravemarkers: Voices of American Culture* (Logan: Utah State University Press, 1992), 293–98.

5. Grant Peckenschneider, "History and Development of Greenwood Cemetery," accessed May 4, 2020, http://www.uni.edu/connors/history.html.

6. "White Bronze Markers More Enduring than Stone," advertisement in *Helena Independent Record*, July 2, 1892.

7. Examples of advertisements for these firms can be found in the *Helena Weekly Herald*, September 5, 1878; *Butte Weekly Miner*, December 28, 1880; *Fort Benton River Press*, March 16, 1881. Dutro was better known for his photography.

8. "Helena Marble Works," *Helena Weekly Herald*, December 29, 1887.

9. "Real Estate Transfers," *Helena Independent Record*, February 8, 1884, and advertisements in the *Helena Weekly Herald*, June 19, 1884. Robert Lang Prescott, unpublished family reminiscence furnished by grandson Jeremiah Hedges Prescott, October 19, 2003. Copy in possession of author. Another unpublished reminiscence by Prescott's son, Harold Bailey Prescott, 1968, offers somewhat conflicting information. MS in possession of the author.

10. "Montana Marble Works," *Helena Independent Record*, April 6, 1890; "Local Notes," *Billings Weekly Gazette*, July 3, 1890. The firm advertised widely in the *Gazette* during 1890.

11. "Tour among the Indians," *New York Times*, June 24, 1872; "U.S. Geological Survey," *Helena Weekly Herald*, July 4, 1872; "Sad News—Sudden Death of the Wife of Sir William Blackmore," *Helena Weekly Herald*, July 25, 1872.

12. Harvey Griffen, "Bozeman's Cemetery Is Place of Peace," *Billings Gazette*,

May 30, 1967; Sunset Hills, accessed May 4, 2020, http://files.usgwarchives .net/mt/gallatin/cemetery/sunsethills.txt.

13. City of Billings, "Mountview History," accessed May 4, 2020, https:// ci.billings.mt.us/100/Cemetery.

14. Zena Beth McGlashan, *Buried in Butte* (Butte MT: Wordz & Ink, 2010), 25, 30–36.

15. Mary Ellen Stubb, "Missoula City Cemetery (1884–Present)," accessed May 4, 2020, https://www.ci.missoula.mt.us/DocumentCenter/View/412 /Missoula-City-Cemetery-History?bidId=.

16. Dorothy Wells, "Forestvale Cemetery," National Register of Historic Places nomination form, 1990, State Historic Preservation Office, Helena, Montana.

17. "Death of Chas. E, Conrad," *Great Falls Tribune*, November 28, 1902.

18. James E. Murphy, *Half Interest in a Silver Dollar: The Saga of Charles E. Conrad* (Missoula MT: Mountain Press, 1983), 231.

19. Murphy, *Half Interest*, 244; personal communication with sexton James Korn, May 18, 2012.

20. Murphy, *Half Interest*, 232.

21. Ellen Baumler, "C.E. Conrad Memorial Cemetery," National Register of Historic Places nomination form, State Historic Preservation Office, Helena, Montana.

9. Cemetery Diversity

1. Vera Haffey, "Superfund to Benefit Anaconda Cemetery," *Montana Standard*, June 21, 2005.

2. See figure 5, chapter 2.

3. Ellen Baumler, "Forgotten Pioneers: The Chinese in Montana," *Montana The Magazine of Western History* 65:2 (Summer 2015), 41–56.

4. "Chinese Bones," *Helena Independent-Record*, October 14, 1881.

5. "Condensed Heathen," the *New North-west*, October 17, 1874.

6. Christopher Merritt, *The Coming Man from Canton* (Lincoln: University of Nebraska, 2017) 241–44.

7. "Chinese Funeral," *Philipsburg Mail*, August 8, 1889.

8. John Ellingsen, former curator of history, Montana Heritage Commission, Virginia City, numerous conversations with the author, 1996–2005; "In Virginia Town," *Madisonian*, April 13, 1895, mentions Wing Dot's burial in the Chinese cemetery.

9. "Local Items: Ah Tong," *Montana Post*, October 28, 1865.

10. "Montana Matters," *Helena Independent*, June 7, 1884.

11. Merritt, *Coming Man from Canton*, 83.

12. Mai Wah Society, "Dr. Huie Pock Practiced Herbal Medicine," *Montana Standard*, October 28, 2014.

13. Mai Wah Society, "Dr. Huie Pock Practiced Herbal Medicine."

14. City of Missoula, "Japanese Railroad Burials," accessed May 4, 2020, https://www.ci.missoula.mt.us/DocumentCenter/View/8242/Japanese -Railroad-Burials?bidId=.

15. Linda Halstead-Acharya, "Fading History," *Billings Gazette*, July 27, 2008.

16. William Toll in Ava A. Kahn, ed., *Jewish Life in the American West* (Berkeley CA: Autry Museum of Western Heritage, 2002), 83.

17. Julie L. Coleman. *Golden Opportunities: A Biographical History of Montana's Jewish Communities* (Helena: Falcon Press, 1994), 22; Birney Hoffman, *Vigilantes* (Philadelphia: Penn Publishing, 1929), 209.

18. Montana Historical Society Map Collection, reprinted in Marilyn Grant, *Main Street Guide to Virginia City* (Helena: Montana Historical Society Press, 1998), 13.

19. Home of Peace Cemetery Association, Records, MC 38, 1865–1843, Montana Historical Society Research Center Archives, Helena, Montana.

20. Ellen Baumler, "Home of Peace Cemetery," National Register of Historic Places nomination, 2006, State Historic Preservation Office, Helena, Montana.

21. Home of Peace Association, Records; *Montana Post*, January 28, 1869; "Sad Bereavement," *Helena Weekly Herald*, January 28, 1869; "The Funeral of Mary Goldman," February 4, 1869.

22. Home of Peace Cemetery Association, Records.

23. Roger Clawson, "Stone Cherubs Tell Bit of History," *Billings Gazette*, May 19, 1985; Mary McCormick, "Gebo Cemetery," National Register of Historic Places nomination, 1993. State Historic Preservation Office, Helena, Montana.

24. McCormick, "Gebo Cemetery."

25. Jon Axline, "Bearcreek Cemetery," National Register of Historic Places nomination, 2011, State Historic Preservation Office, Helena, Montana.

26. Little Bighorn Battlefield National Monument, National Park Service, accessed May 4, 2020, https://www.nps.gov/libi/planyourvisit/custer -national-cemetery.htm.

27. Military Salute Project, Military and Veterans Protocol, "Placing Coins on Headstones," accessed May 4, 2020, http://militarysalute.proboards.com /thread/864/placing-coins-on-headstones.

28. "Local News," *Helena Weekly Herald*, July 18, 1872.

29. Kate Hampton, "Lewis and Clark County Hospital Historic District," National Register nomination, 2002, State Historic Preservation Office, Helena, Montana.

30. Justin Post, "Cemetery for Poor Is Reminder of Butte's Past," *Montana Standard*, May 29, 2010.

31. Lorna Thackeray, "Poor Farm Was 'Safety Net,'" *Billings Gazette*, September 2, 1996.

32. City of Missoula, "Missoula Burial Sites (1800s–Present)," accessed May 4, 2020, http://www.ci.missoula.mt.us/DocumentCenter/Home/View/29762.

33. Montana State University, "Montana Body Donation Program." Accessed May 4, 2020. www.montana.edu/wwami/mbdp/.

10. Homage to the Dead

1. "Butte's Night of Horror," *Anaconda Standard*, January 16, 1895.

2. "Butte's Night of Horror," *Anaconda Standard*.

3. "Laid to Rest," *Butte Miner*, January 18, 1895.

4. "With Solemn Ceremony," *Butte Miner*, January 19, 1895.

5. Zena Beth McGlashan, *Buried in Butte* (Butte MT: Wordz & Ink, 2010), 288–89.

6. "Tribute to Noble Chieftain," *Billings Gazette*, March 18, 1932.

7. "Plenty Coups Rites Held at Pryor Tuesday," *Billings Gazette*, March 9, 1932.

8. "Last of Great Chieftains of Indians Laid to Rest Amid Tribal Ceremonies," *Montana Standard*, March 9, 1932.

9. Extracted from the National Register marker written by the author in 2016.

10. "City Will Pay Last Tribute to C. M. Russell Today," *Great Falls Tribune*, October 27, 1926.

11. "Montana Mourns at Charlie Russell's Grave," *Great Falls Tribune*, October 28, 1926.

12. Jon Emeigh, *MTN News*, November 25, 2019, https://www.kpax.com/news/first-part-of-memorial-erected-in-honor-of-butte-firefighters-killed-in-historic-warehouse-explosion.

13. Gates of the Mountains, "Mann Gulch Fire," accessed May 4, 2020, http://www.gatesofthemountains.com/area-history/mann-gulch-fire/.

14. Waymarking, "Hebgen Lake Earthquake," https://www.waymarking.com/waymarks/WMCQKN_Hebgen_Lake_Earthquake.

15. Baumler, *More Montana Moments*, 72–73.

16. Author conversation with Irene Bowker, August 2012.

17. "Faithful Shep, Hit by Train," *Great Falls Tribune*, January 13, 1942; "Funeral Held for Shep at Fort Benton," *Great Falls Tribune*, January 15, 1942; "Grave Monument to Perpetuate Memory of Faithful Sheep Dog," *Great Falls Tribune*, January 19, 1942; "Shep Dies Still Waiting for Master's Return," *Great Falls Tribune*, January 25, 1942.

18. Leslie McCartney, "Sculpture Planned for Famous Mutt," *Montana Standard*, November 21, 2003; Thad Kelling, "Auditor Memorial Complete," *Montana Standard*, April 28, 2005; Baumler, *Montana Moments*, 2–3.

19. Baumler, *Montana Moments*, 5; "Boomer is Dead," (photograph caption), *Great Falls Tribune*, February 21, 1949; Waymarking, "Smoking Boomer Rail Trail," accessed May 4, 2020, https://www.waymarking.com/waymarks/WM107TD_Smoking_Boomer_Rail_Trail_Harlowton_MT.

20. Ellen Baumler, "Old Pitt," *Montana Moments* (blog), August 20, 2012, https://ellenbaumler.blogspot.com/2012/08/old-pitt.html; Jack Kirkley, "Pitt Is Remembered," *Dillon Tribune*, August 4, 1993; Kirkley, "Pitt," *Dillon Tribune*, August 11, 1993.

21. "Marker Erected in Memory of Circus Elephant," *Dillon Daily Tribune*, November 22, 1943.

11. How We Miss Them

1. Jessie M. Shawyer and Fern E. Schillreff, *Garfield County, the Golden Years* (Jordan, MT: n.p., 1969), 40–42.

2. *Helena Independent-Record*, May 29, 1875.

3. "Not Many Buried Alive," *Anaconda Standard*, October 19, 1897, reprinted from the *New York Times*.

4. Casket in American usage refers to a four-sided receptacle, while a coffin is the more old-fashioned six-sided wooden box.

5. Gary Laderman, *Rest in Peace: A Cultural History of Death and the Funeral Home in the Twentieth Century* (New York: Oxford University Press, 2003), 6–8.

6. Cremation Association of North America, "Industry Statistical Information," accessed May 2, 2020, https://www.cremationassociation.org/page/IndustryStatistics.

7. Mary McCormick and Joan Brownell, "Red Lodge Mausoleum," National Register of Historic Places nomination, 2011, State Historic Preservation Office, Helena, Montana.

8. "A Sad Death," *Helena Independent-Record*, July 23, 1889.

9. "Thomas Thexton Convicted," *Anaconda Standard*, March 23, 1906.

10. "Ironic Tombstone Erected Over Grave of Desperado Found after Long Search," *Helena Independent Record*, May 16, 1937.

11. McGlashan, *Buried in Butte*, 298.

12. "Memorial Proceedings on the Death of Hon. Oscar A. Sedman," *Helena Weekly Herald*, February 17, 1881.

13. Annette Stott, *Pioneer Cemeteries and Sculpture Gardens of the Old West* (Lincoln: University of Nebraska, 2008), 280.

14. "A Sudden Death," *Philipsburg Mail*, March 19, 1896.

15. Mike Koop, "Mountain View Cemetery," National Register of Historic Places nomination, 1987. State Historic Preservation Office, Helena, Montana.

16. "Personal," *New North-west*, April 26, 1878.

Bibliographic Essay

Cemetery research must begin with site visits, but there are finding aids and essential resources that quickly and efficiently enhance the search for the dead. Findagrave.com, Ancestry.com, and Newspapers.com are the three most critical resources on the web. Find a Grave includes comprehensive inventories of most of Montana's recorded cemeteries, many photos of individual tombstones, and often includes published obituaries. While not all states provide public access to death certificates and other legal documents, this information is available for Montana through Ancestry. These three online resources are accessible through private subscription or through many local libraries.

Newspapers are especially helpful because they often include detailed obituaries. Free online newspapers specific to Montana include https://chroniclingamerica.loc.gov/, which features both Montana and national newspapers and the *Montana Post*. A rich collection of small-town Montana newspapers can be accessed at http://montananewspapers.org/. These searchable resources not only provide information about individuals, but also often provide details about the founding of local cemeteries, the moving of graves, and the discovery of human remains.

Although county histories may or may not directly mention cemeteries, community context is essential in understanding their development. County histories can also be helpful when researching individual family histories. Many county histories have been digitized and are accessible online through the Montana Memory Project at https://mtmemory.org/digital/collection

/p15018coll43/search/. The earliest Montana history, county by county, is Michael A. Leeson's *History of Montana 1739–1885* (Chicago: Warner, Beers, 1885), available online at several websites. Subscription histories, such as *Progressive Men of the State of Montana* (Chicago: A. W. Bowen and Company, 1903), can provide personal information and are valuable resources.

Historical overviews are also important for Montana context. The best general history of Montana before Euro-American contact is Douglas H. MacDonald's *Montana Before History: 11,000 Years of Hunter Gatherers in the Rockies and Plains* (Missoula MT: Mountain Press, 2012). A classic Native American cultural history is John C. Ewers' *The Blackfeet: Raiders on the Northwestern Plains* (Norman: University of Oklahoma, 1958) 106–7. The standard nineteenth and twentieth Montana history is Michael P. Malone, Richard B. Roeder, William Lang's *Montana: A History of Two Centuries*, rev ed. (Seattle: University of Washington, 1991).

National Register of Historic Places nominations require a tremendous amount of research. Cemetery nominations include a history of the community, detailed history of the cemetery, extensive bibliographies, photographs, and maps. These are valuable documents housed at the Montana State Historic Preservation Office, under the auspices of the Montana Historical Society. The SHPO website is at https://mhs.mt.gov/Shpo. Nominations can be accessed through that office and many of them can also be found online.

Charleen Spalding's exemplary work in Broadwater, Lewis and Clark, and Jefferson counties includes inventories of nearly every known cemetery in the tricounty area and lists of those interred in the more obscure burial grounds. The information is available to the public at the Montana Historical Society's Research Center. Her book, *Benton Avenue Cemetery: A Pioneer Resting Place* (Helena MT: Pioneer Tales Publishing, 2010), is a great model for those wanting to write about individual cemeteries. Similarly, Zena Beth McGlashan's monumental work, *Buried in Butte* (Butte MT: Wordz & Ink, 2010), includes histories of all Butte's cemeteries as well cultural histories and anecdotes.

Finally, Annette Stott's *Pioneer Cemeteries: Sculpture Gardens of the Old West* (Lincoln: University of Nebraska, 2008) is a wonderful cultural and visual synopsis of the development of funerary art and artistry in the Rocky Mountain region and includes numerous Montana examples.

Index

Page numbers in italics indicate illustrations.

Adams, Louis, xv, xx

African Americans, 19, 66, 105, 107, 109, 148

Alder Gulch, 69, 111, 116

Alkali Creek, 33, 34, 37, 40

Allen, Roscoe F., 40

Allen, William Alonzo, 37

American Fur Company, 14, 25–27, 61

American Legion, 158–59

Anaconda, 29, 79, 99, 106, 118

Anzick Site, 2, 3, 5, 11

Appell, Jonathon, xix

A-Ra-Poo-Ash, 19

Assiniboine, 13, 14, 15, 25 27

Auditor, 139

Axline, Jon, xx

Bach, Gussie, 148

Bad Wound, 16–17

Baker, Eugene M., 28

Bannack, 43, 44, 66, *68*, 68–69, 71, 73, 74, 115

battles. *See individual battlefields*

Baumler, Katie and Mark, xx

Beachy, Hill, 44

Bearcreek Cemetery, xx, 134, 151, *152*

Beckwourth, James, 19–20

Bell, William H., 68–69, 73, 105

bells at grave sites, 143, *144*

Benevolent Protective Order of Elks, 37, 149

Benton Avenue Cemetery (Spalding), xix, *178*

Benton Avenue Cemetery (Helena), xvi, 87, 100, 148–49, 153–54

Bering (Beringian) Land Bridge, 1, 3, 22

Berkley Pit, 137, 139

Beth Aaron Cemetery (Billings), 118

Bickford, Sarah, 107

Big Hole National Battlefield Monument, 51–55, *55*, 59

Big Hole River, 52

Big Timber, 89–90

Billings, xii, 7, 30, 33–41, 74–75, 97–99, 118, 124, 130–31, 147

Billings Bison Trap, 33, 35

Bird, Evangeline, 88

Bison antiquus, 3

Bitterroot Valley, 20, 52, 63

Black Death, 27

Blackfeet, 15–18, *19*, 23, 27, 28, *31*, *38*, 39, 46, 54–55, 61, 65, 108

Blackmore, William and Mary, 98

B'nai Israel Cemetery (Butte), 118

Bogert, Elizabeth, and John, 98

Boot Hill (Bannack), *68*, 68–69

Boot Hill (Helena), 73, 84

Boot Hill (Virginia City), 70–71

Boot Hill Cemetery (Coulson), 35, 40, 75, 166n1

"box" interment, 20

Boyd Cemetery (Libby), 78

Boyle, Hugh, 56

Bozeman, xii–xiii, 97–98, 108, 126, 154

Bradley, James, 18, 34–35, 37, 39, 47, 49–50, 53

Bridgewater, Samuel, 66

Brotherhood of American Yeomen, 106

buffalo robes, and contagion, 27

burial laws, 10–12

Butte, 29, 52, 95, 97, 99–100, 110, *111*, 113, 117–18, 123–24, 127–28, 132–34, 137–39, 149, *150*, 153, 157

Butte Warehouse Explosion, 127–28, 132, 133–34, 139

cairn burials, 4, 51

Calloway, Lew, 71

Calvary Cemetery (Havre), 107

Camelops hesternus, 3

Cameron, Angus, 128

cannibalism, 9–10

carbon dating. *See* radiocarbon dating

Cass, Lewis, 27

Catholicism, 20–21

cats, 15

C. E. Conrad Memorial Cemetery, *103*, 101–4

Cemetery Island (Canyon Ferry), 77

Central School (Helena), *74*, 84, 148

Cheyenne, 8, 13, 17, 35, 56. *See also* Northern Cheyenne

children's graves, 75, *76*, 119, 122–23, *152*, 153–54, 157

China Row (Helena), 110–11

Chinese and Chinese burials customs, 15, 82, 108–13, *111*

Chinese Exclusion Act, 109, 112, 113

Chippewa, 24

Christianity, 21–22, 145

Civil War, 120, 130, 144

Clancy, 85–87, *86*

Clark, William A., 113, 157, *158*

Clarke, Malcolm, 28

Clovis culture, 2–3

coffin hardware, 82–83, *83*

coins on tombstones, 121

Cole Brothers Circus, 140

Comanche, 49. *See also* horses

Congregation Beth Aaron (Billings), 118

Connor, Stu, 166n8

Conrad, Alicia "Lettie," 101–4

Conrad, Charles, 101

Consolidated Mausoleum Company, 147

consumption. *See* tuberculosis

contagion, 28–32, 67

Content, Solomon, 116

Copeland, William, 139

Corvallis Cemetery, 148

Coulson, 34–35, *35*, 37, 74–75

COVID-19, 31

cremation, 18, 142, 145, 150

Crittenden, J. J., 47, *48*

crosses, xii, 60, 75, 119, 134, *154*, 155, 158–59, *160*

Crow, 6, 8, 13, 16–17, 18–19, 27, 33–35, 37, 39, 45, 51, 129–30

Crow Agency, 120

Crowley, Eddy, 30

Cruse, Thomas, 146

Culbertson, Alexander, 26

Custer, George Armstrong, 46–47

Custer National Cemetery (Hardin), 47–48, 65–66, 120, *121*

Cyrillic tombstones, 119, 151, *152*

Dalton family, 70–71, 169n13

Davis, Les, 5

Dawson County Cemetery (Glendive), 147

Dearborn Crossing Cemetery, 77–78

Deer Lodge, xiv–xv, 52–53, *114*, 115, 116, 122, 146, 154, 157, *158*

Demersville, 63, 95, 101

Denig, Edwin Thompson, 14

De Smet, Pierre-Jean, 64

Diamond City Cemetery, 77–78

Dillon, 87–89, 140

Dillon, "Charity" Jane, 80

Dimsdale, Thomas, 72

diphtheria, 23, 67, 75, *76*

diseases. *See individual diseases*

disfigurement, 23, 28

dogs, 15, 17, 26, 28, 34, 88, 136–39, *138*

Dolan, Jim, 139

Doolittle, Craig, xx, 86

Dorman, Isaiah, 49

Dudley, William, 75

Eahart, Floyd, 158

Earp, Celestia Alice, xii–xiii

earth burial, 15, 18, 142, 145, 147

Elk City ID, 43

Elkhorn, 74–76, *76*

embalming, 142–45

enclosures, of grave sites, 157

epidemics, 23–30, 34–39, 65, 67, 91–92, 145

epitaphs, xii–xiii, 76, 113, 119, 123, 142, 148–49, 153–54

"Ever Faithful," 137, *138*

exhumation, 11, 90, 109

Ezekiel, Ben, 115, 116

"Face on the Rims," xii, *36*, 36–37

Fairview Cemetery (Richland County), 107

Fairy Steps, 102–3, *103*

Far West (steamboat), 49

Fatality Safety Marker Program, 158–59, *160*

fencing. *See* enclosures

Flathead Indian Reservation, 63, 65

flowers, 118, 131–32, 143, 157, 159

Forestvale Cemetery (Helena), 66, 89, 98, 100–101, 104, 110, 123, 147, 153

Fort Belknap Reservation, *21*, 108

Fort Benton, 60, 61–63, 65, 77, 84, 95, 136–37, *138*

Fort Clark ND, 24

Fort Connah, 60–61, 95, 143, *144*

Fort Harrison, 66

Fort Keogh, 66

Fort Logan, 66

Fort McKenzie, 25, 27

Fort Missoula, 53

Fort Missoula Post Cemetery, 66, 120

Fort Owen, 63

Fort Peck Dam, 135

Fort Peck Reservation, 30, 31

Fort Shaw, 65

Fort Union ND, 14, 24–25, 26, 27

Fraternal Order of Eagles, 106, 149

fraternal organizations. *See specific names*

Frenchtown, 63

funerary rituals, 17–22, 143

Garcia, Andrew, 53–54

"garden park" cemeteries, 93, 104

Gates of the Mountains Wilderness, 134

Gebo Cemetery (Fromberg), 118–19

German Gulch, 110

German-Russian Catholics, 119

Ghost Cave, 8

Gibbon, General John, 47, 52

Glendive, 6, 147

Goldman, Mary, 117

gold rush, xiv, 42–45, 67–68, 73, 94, 105, 108–9, 115

Granite Mountain/Speculator Mine, xii, 132–33, *133*, 134, 139, 149

Grasshopper Creek, 43, 68

Great Falls, 28, 30, 118, 131, *132*, 147

Great Falls Hebrew Association, 118

Great Northern Railway, 78, 102, 113

Greycliff, 45, 46

Gros Ventre, 27

Hagen Site, 6–7, 39

Harvey family, 87

Head Chief, 56–58

Hebrew Benevolent Society, 116

Hebrew Cemetery (Virginia City), 116

Helena, xiii, xvi, 66, 73–74, *74*, 84–85, 95–97, 100–101, 110, 116–17, 123, 146, 148–49, 151, 153

Hell Gate, 62, 81

Highland Cemetery (Great Falls), 131–32

Hillcrest Cemetery (Deer Lodge), xiv, *114*, 115, 122, 146, 154, 157, *158*

Hillside Cemetery (Virginia City), *ii*, 70–73, 72, *96*, 107, 148

Hobert, Arthur W., 102

Home of Peace Cemetery (Helena), xiii, 116–17

horses, 7, 13, 15–17, *16*, 24, 26, 28, 34, 47, 49, *50*, 57, 66, 78, 87, 117, 127, 131, *132*, 148

Horsethief State Park WA, 37

Howard, O. O., 52

Hudson's Bay Company, 61

Hughes, Cheryl, xv, xx

human bone. *See* human remains

human remains, 8, 10–12, 30, 48, 52, 79–90

Hutterite cemeteries, 107

Immel, Michael, 39–40

Improved Order of Red Men, 106

Independent Order of Oddfellows, 106, 149

Indian Rock, 40

Indian Vaccination Act, 27

influenza, 30–32, 155

In-who-lise, 54

Iron Jaw Wilcox Site, 4

Ives, George, 70, 115

Jacobs, Michael, 155, *156*

Japanese, 113–15, *114*

Jefferson County, 85–86

Jenner, Edward, 26

Jews, 105, 108, 115–18

Jocko Agency Cemetery (Arlee), xv, xx, 108

Johnston, Jennie, 88–89

Jones, Robert, 39

Kalispell, xvii, 63, 98, 101–4, *103*, 107

Kalispell (tribe), 64

Kelly, Luther Sage "Yellowstone," 130–31

Kelly Mountain, 36

Keogh, Myles, 49

Kirkendall, Hugh, 53

Knights of Columbus, 106

Knights of Pythias, 106

Kooistra, Kevin, 36

Kootenai, 64

Krieg, Fred, 40

Lake County, 60–61, 64, 108, *144*

Lakewood Cemetery (Minneapolis), 102

Lakota language, 49

Lakota Sioux, 14, 46. *See also* Cheyenne

Lambert, Kirby, xix

Lame Deer, 57

Lane, George, 70–72

Larpenteur, Charles, 25

Last Act of the Sioux War, 16

Last Chance. *See* Helena

Last Stand Hill, 48

lawn cemeteries, 93

Le Moyne, Francis, 145

Lewis, Oscar T., 7–8, *9*

Lewis and Clark Corps of Discovery, 23

Lewiston ID, 43–44

Libby Cemetery, 78

Lienesch, John, 46

Lim, Lee Foo, 82, 110

Little, Frank, 149, *150*

Little Bighorn Battlefield National Monument, 46–51, *48, 50,* 65

Little Dog, 28

Logan, Captain William, 53–55

Long Hair, 20

Long Horse, 18–19

Lutheran Cemetery (Melville), 107

MacDonald family, 61, 95, 143, *144*

maggots, 25, 53

Magruder, Lloyd, 42–45

Magruder Road Corridor, 45, 58

Mahoney Ranch, 5

Mandan, 7, 24

Mann Gulch, 134, *135*

Masonic Cemetery (Twin Bridges), 105–6

Masons, 69, 90, 99, 105, 106, 149, 168n9

Mausoleums, 93, 102–3, 145–47

Mayn Cemetery (White Sulphur Springs),
 154, 154–55

McGill, Caroline, xiii

McGuire, James, 54, *55*

McWhirk family, 83

measles, 23, 67, 78, 84, 151

Medicine Crow, Joe, 133–34, 166n1

memorial park cemeteries, 93, 104

Métis, 61, 62

Metra Park (Billings), 34

Miles City, 66, 120

Milk River Valley Church of the Brethren
 Cemetery (Kremlin), 107

Milwaukee Railroad, 113, 139

Missoula, 28, 62, 80–83, *81, 83,* 84, 110, 113, 115,
 120, 124, 134, 158

Missoula City Cemetery, 100–101, 114

Missoula City Cemetery (old), 81–83, *81, 83*

Missoula Marble Works, 95, 97

Missouri Fur Company, 39–41

Mitchell, Deb, xix

Mitchell, Armistead and Hugh, xiv–xv

Montana Body Donation Program, 125–26

Montana Historical Society, xix, 3, 161

Montana History Foundation, xix, 161

Montana Sandstone Company, 155

Montana School of Mines, 8

Montana State Hospital (Warm Springs),
 xii–xv, 124, *125*

Montana State Orphans Home, 122

Montana Veterans' Home Cemetery (Columbia Falls), 120

Morony Mausoleum, 146

mortuary customs, 13–22

Mountain View Cemetery (Big Timber), 90

Mountain View Cemetery (Butte), 133, *133,* 149

Mountain View Cemetery (Columbus), 155, *156*

Mountain View Cemetery (Dillon), 87–89

Mount Auburn Cemetery (Cambridge MA), 92–93, 97
Mount Jumbo, 81, *81*
Mount Moriah Cemetery (Butte), 97, 99, 111, *111*, 113, 128, 133, 149, *150*, 153
Mountview Cemetery (Billings), 97, 98–99
Mullan Road, 65
Mulloy, William, 6–7, 10
Mussigbrod, Charles F., xiv

National Cemetery Act, 120
Native American Graves Protection and Repatriation Act (NAGPRA), 11, 72
Nevada City MT, 44, 69–70, 115
Nevada City Cemetery, 70, 151
Nez Perce, 51–55, 61
Nez Perce Pass, xv, 43, 44
Nez Perce Trail, 43
Norris, Philetus W., 18
Northern Cheyenne, 11, 56. *See also* Cheyenne
Northern Pacific Railway, 60
Noxon, 112

ochre, 1–5, 7, 22, 30
O'Donnell family, 99
Old Coyote, Henry, 33–34
Old Pitt, 140

Paint, 16–17. *See also* horses
Peel, Langford, 149
Pend d' Oreille, 64
Père Lachaise Cemetery (Paris, France), 92
"pest camps," 29
Petrosa, Pasqual, 155, *156*
Pictograph Cave, 7–10, *9*
Piegan (Blackfeet), 25–26, 28, 55
Place of the Skulls, 33–39
"Place Where the White Horse Went Down," 34–39
Pleasant, Alice "Ma Plaz," 107
Plenty Coups, 129–30, *130*
pneumonia, 24, 45, 62, 78, 98, 141, 154
Pock, Huie, 112–13
Pococke, L. Rodney, 73, 84
Poindexter family, 88–89
poor farms, 123–24
Porsild, Charlene, xix
portraits on tombstones, 151, *152*
Power, T. C., 146

Pre-Contact period, 5, 6, 7
Prescott, Alonzo K., 95–97, *96*, 153

Quake Lake, 135

radiocarbon dating, 2, 4, 8
Red Lodge City Cemetery, 147
Resurrection Cemetery (Helena), 85, 146
Ringling family, 154
River Crow, 19, 33–34
Riverside Cemetery (Billings), 24
Riverside Cemetery (Fort Benton), 62, 124
Rixon, Harold, 40
Robinson, Jabez, 72, 72–73
Robinson Park (Helena), 85, 170n12
Rocky Mountain Elk Foundation, 81
Rocky Mountain spotted fever, 67
Roundup, 106
Row, Charles F., 47
rural garden cemeteries, 93, 102, 104
Russell, C. M. "Charlie," 16–17, 131–32, *132*

Sacred Heart Catholic Cemetery (Fort Belknap), *21*, 108
Sacrifice Cliff, 36, 166n3
Salish, xv, 13, 20–21, 64, *64*
Salmon River ID, 43
Sanders, Wilbur, 148–49
Saukamappee, 23
Sayre, Henry Melville, 8–10
scaffold burial, 14–15, *16*, 17–18, 30, 51, 81
Schanche, Tony, 136
Schrader, Jimmy Duane, 155
Schwab family, *153*, 154
Sedman, Oscar, 151
Selway-Bitterroot Wilderness, xv, 45
Seventh Cavalry, 46–47, 49
Shep, 136–37, *138*
"She Who Watches." *See* Tsagiglala
Shields, G. O., 54
Shodair Children's Hospital, 123
Sioux, 8, 13, 15, *16*, 18, 24, 45–51
Sisters of Providence, 65
skeletal remains. *See* human remains
Skeleton Cliff. *See* Place of the Skulls
Sligh family, 153
smallpox, 23–32, 34
Smith Mine disaster (Bearcreek), 119, 134

Smoking Boomer, 139–40

Spalding, Charleen, xix, 80, 178

Spanish "flu," 32, 113, 118

Split-Rock Burial, 4–6

State Board of Health, 29–30

St. Ignatius Mission, 63–65

St. John Berchman's Catholic Church (Jocko Agency), xv, 108

St. John the Baptist Cemetery (Frenchtown), 63

St. Mary's Catholic Cemetery on Oakes (Helena). See Robinson Park

St. Mary's Mission, 20–21, 63–64, 64, 95

St. Olaf Church Cemetery (Red Lodge), 107

Stott, Annette, 179

St. Patrick's Catholic Cemetery (Butte), 128

St. Peter (steamboat), 24–26

Stuart, Granville, 53, 55

suicide, 27–28, 34–36, 56–57

Sunset Hills Cemetery (Bozeman), 98, 108, 126

Taylor, Jack, 107, 148

Tbalt, Nicholas, 70

territorial prison (Deer Lodge), 122

Thibadeau, Mathilda. See Dalton family

Thomas family massacre, 45–46, 80

Thompson, David, 23–24

Three Forks of the Missouri, 26

tombstone adornments, 148–57

tombstone makers, 94–97

toolkit, 3–4, 5, 22

tree burials, 37–39, 38

tree trunks, ii, 155–57, 156

Tsagiglala, 37

tuberculosis, 73, 83, 89, 122

Twin Bridges Cemetery, 122–23

United Mine Workers of America, 106, 120

Upper Hill Cemetery (Anaconda), 106

Upper Missouri tribes, 13–28

urns, 150–51

Ursuline Sisters, 65

Van Orsdel, William Wesley "Brother Van," 88–89

Victor, Chief, 21

vigilantes, 44–45, 69–70, 73, 85, 115

Virginia City MT, 69–73, 111–12

Wagner, Glendolin Damon, 9–10

Walsh, Thomas, 146

Warm Springs State Hospital, xiii–xiv, 124, 125

Wheeler, Harry V., 100

White, John, 107

White Cross Program. See American Legion

Whitehorn, Clark, xx

White Sulphur Springs, 66, 154–55, 154

whooping cough, 65–66

Wilsall, 1

Wilson, Fern Marie, xvi–xvii

Wimsett monument, 155, 156

Wing Dot, 111–12

Woodmen of the World, 106, 149, 155

Yellowstone National Cemetery (Laurel), 120

Young, John, 17–18

Young Mule, 56–57

Zerbinatti, Pietro, 63

Zimmerman, Joseph, 40

zinc tombstones, 94–95

Zortman, Peter, 89–90